Prepublication Review Copy

Title: Unspoken Thoughts Of A Man™
An intimate journey through expressions of love

Author: Kennedy F. Jones
Category: Relationship/Poetry
Pages: 160
Size: 5.25 x 7
Binding: Hardcover
Illustrations: 33 Full-color

Release date: February 1, 2009
Price: $24.95
ISBN: 978-0-9793710-0-4
LCCN: 2007923513
First Printing: 5,523 copies

Notes:

Distribution arrangments is planned with Baker and Taylor.
Please send a copy of your review to:

IdentiFacts Publications
P.O. Box 16172
Kansas City, MO 64132
816-444-2872

A Loving Gift for

_____

My Suggestion:

☐ Start by reading the back of the cover first.

☐ Read my favorites first; then read the back cover.

My favorites: **page:**

_____   _____

_____   _____

_____   _____

Special thoughts about you:

_____

_____

_____

Date: _____   **From:** _____

UNSPOKEN THOUGHTS OF A MAN ™

An Intimate Journey Through Expressions of Love

By

Kennedy F. Jones

www.kennedyjones.net
IdentiFacts Publications
Kansas City, Missouri

Designed by: Kennedy F. Jones
Printed in the United States of America
ISBN: 978-0-9793710-0-4
LCCN: 2007923513

Acknowledgement

Defining the Man of Love™ is my interpretation of the Holy Scriptures taken
from I Corinthians 13:4 – 7 and Galatians 5:22, 23. I am grateful to be able to
expound on the wisdom that will never become obsolete and will always prove
beneficial to every man and woman who yields to it.

2008-001

Remembering Your Spirit of Phi·li´a
My Beloved Friend

I heard your voice in the chorus of my concerto. Your voice ascended because of its beautiful depth of feeling and was a perfect complement to the music of my love. I will never forget the intensity and outpouring of emotions you felt as your voice became one with your heart. The expressions of your feelings inspired me to reach deeper within myself. Thank you for your beauty; it will always live on in my heart.

Your encouragement and willingness to comment on my work is itself proof of your affection for me. I will always appreciate you, and want to say "thank you" for supporting and believing in me. The role that you play in my life sustains me, and I value the friendship that we have formed. I value the interchange that we have shared over the years. You are an exceptional woman, and I feel honored to have known you. This is my tribute to you, because I will never forget your love for me. Whenever you read this, know that there will always be a place for you within my heart.

I Loved You Before We Met

This book is dedicated to my future wife. The content of this letter is intentionally missing, because it was written for the eyes of my future wife alone. Its purpose is to serve as a reminder that there is no limitation in the amount of love which can exist between us.

Table of Contents

III. A Season of Change

IV. In The End, Love Prevails

Preface

Love is one of those perplexities of life that most men and women cannot seem to find contentment in, nor have they been able to fully comprehend the needs of each other. So inadvertently, the constant pursuit of love has left many hearts in despair. Although the concept of  love is quite simple, it has proven to be complex and elusive in rewards, because the majority of people fail to implement the experience properly. This is primarily due to a lack of knowledge of what actually constitutes the meaning of real love. Added to this are the hardening of the hearts of people to listen to proper guidance and the lack of self-discipline to deny themselves the instant gratification of indulging in licentious behavior. Therefore, as a result of pursuing love on their own terms, it has left both genders, in particular women, with a damaged conscience, low self-esteem, and a lack of self-respect.

For many women, trying to communicate varying degrees of uncertainties within their relationships have left them despondent towards men. Inherently, every woman feels these uncertainties and needs reassurance. Even women with exceptional beauty have fallen victim to the effects of their insecurities, which, in a sense, are like bandits holding them hostage. By wanting freedom from feeling alone, women are steadily crying out to men to rescue their love by simply giving them special attention and to share with them expressions of love and encouragement. However, since their cries for help have gone unanswered, many women feel that men are either just not capable of expressing themselves in the manner they desire or that they simply do not care about their feelings. Contrary to the latter belief, but acknowledging the former, many men do care; they are simply perplexed in trying to solve the constant "emotional mystery" surrounding what women really need.

❋ cont.

In unraveling the "emotional mystery," this book presents an opportunity for me to restore a woman's confidence in a man's ability to understand her concerns, express his feelings, and fulfill the emotional deprivation that exists within themselves. I offer encouragement, inspiration, and hope to all women, because far too many couples are living in loveless marriages. Many are staying together for the sake of convenience only; yet, their hearts are so far removed that there is no sanctity in their union. Sadly, the high divorce rate has become the clearest indication that most men and women do not know what real love is. The emotional disconnect also confirms that many couples do not even know how to express their love in the manner that appeals to their mate.

The manner of love is so important that this book addresses issues that are pertinent to both men and women. It outlines the definition of real love and the character of a man who is working towards displaying it so that a woman may thoroughly examine her own standard of love. This is a timely subject since so many women use poor judgment in selecting their mates. I believe this is primarily due to women becoming so focused on the goal of getting married or so afraid of being alone that they ignore all of the warning signs, and commit to a long-term relationship that leads to their detriment. Eventually, the valley of despair is where a woman will go to find refuge to lament her decisions, and in her sorrow, she will cry out for strength and relief from her heartache. Unfortunately, she cannot always find for herself a source of refreshment that will rejuvenate her spirit of love—that is, until now.

This book provides a woman with refreshment, because it represents more than just a book of poetry or the mushy sentiments of a man. It is therapy for the soul of both the young maiden and the woman of advanced years. Since the feeling of love never becomes passe to either one, the expressions within this book will always have a place in their lives. This book uses intimate thoughts of love as a means of healing and teaching by using poetry, essays, and love letters as its vessel to appeal to the heart of a woman and to have her reflect deeply about her life. Are men always to blame, or does she share some responsibility? Without provoking her, the strength of this book uses the softness of a feather to help her answer this question and others that are similar. This book is also a servant that builds rapport, dispels certain myths about men, and encourages her to release the negative feelings and aspire to become the woman of her own choosing. This comforting inspiration and counsel is nouveau to a woman in that this type of love springs forth from an unlikely source—the feelings of a man! Yes, the feelings of a man in whom she thought they could not possibly exist! Yet, here they are.

In reading this book, I would like to suggest that you start from the beginning without skipping certain parts to reach the end. While this book is not meant to be read like a typical novel, each piece individually stands alone but contributes to a unity of thought that is an integral and essential part of the collective theme. Although this book is primarily for women, there are many lessons that men can learn. The man who is willing to read this book can gain insight into what a woman means when she asks him to talk to her about his feelings. Thus, the great "emotional mystery" is solvable, and, to simplify the answer, I will just candidly tell you what it means.

The basis of understanding the "emotional mystery" and interacting with a woman is not that complicated. Very simply, what primarily matters to a woman is not a man's level of accomplishments, or his economic or social status; rather, a woman always wants to feel loved. She wants to feel needed and appreciated by the man in her life. A woman also wants the benefits of a monogamous relationship and the emotional security of being with a man who does not masquerade in accepting it, but, who will cherish the value of it. No matter the culture, race, or nationality, a woman is always a woman despite the exterior, because the emotional interior always needs a delicate balance of attention from the man she loves.

I submit to you that a woman listens intently to a man who speaks about love and will open her heart to receive him, if, he directs his attention towards her. I also submit to you that no woman feels that the strength of a man's character diminishes by his ability to show loving kindness towards her; rather, a woman is infused by his attention and views it as an enhancement! Acts of appreciation such as opening her door, assisting with her coat, complimenting her looks, and saying "thank you" are high standards of propriety that a man should strive never to compromise. Even when conversing with her, he should strive to keep his speech free from vulgarity or rudeness. A man with extraordinary refinement continues to show love, kindness, and decency towards his woman. I firmly believe that no other substitute encapsulates a man's love when he speaks to his woman from his heart. I believe in order to maintain her confidence in love, a definitive line must be established that sets a standard of excellence in a man's conduct and speech. Furthermore, it should be unacceptable for a woman to accept anything below that line of expectation.

In an effort to raise the standard of excellence by example, this book also presents an opportunity for me to affirm a woman's confidence in a man's ability to express his love in a clean and honorable manner. This book sets a benchmark that there are unlimited ways for a man to express affection without degrading intimacy. For my part, I desire to exceed a woman's standard of excellence in presenting my interpretation of love. By engaging her thoughts and feelings in a genteel manner, I hope to capture the essence of her love and inspire her with the profound beauty of a man.

Experiencing real love is a gift of life that very few people have had the pleasure of knowing. If you are one of the few, then you are truly blessed. For I believe that you can indeed miss what you do not have, and those persons privileged to have experienced the beauty of real love understand that it is priceless, even if it is for a brief moment in time.

To the Distinguished Gentleman

As a man matures, he reaches a point when he looks back and reflects on his successes and failures in life. In most cases, he realizes that he was able to reach his full potential due to the aid of the woman in his life, or he senses a void that makes him feel incomplete without her. In the former case, the behind-the-scenes contributions a woman makes on behalf of the man she loves often go unnoticed and unappreciated, but her sacrifices add immense value to his life. A woman who is capable in respect to the duties women customarily perform is a pearl of high value and is worthy of praise. I hope that you are able to recognize such a remarkable woman who is suited to your personality and that you treat her accordingly. By reading this book, it will not only add to your insight, but its expressions can assist you in your efforts. Think of this book as a template that you can use as a starting point to help you into putting your own thoughts into words that will appeal to the makeup of your woman.

If you are already very affectionate and attentive to your woman, then I commend your efforts and encourage you to continue doing so. As one gentleman to another, may I offer a reminder to the wise? There exists a universal trait among women from the beginning of their creation which has transcended to our time. Namely, a woman needs to know, a woman needs to feel secure in knowing that her man loves only her today and will love only her tomorrow. It is true that the little things mean the most. Expensive gifts or extravagant fanfares of affection cannot compare to a man who is willing to talk intimately with his woman and is open in sharing his fears, his dreams, and aspirations. Simple pleasures build a firm foundation. Simplicity brings out the best in love.

An Invitation to Women

As a woman, you do not need me to explain to you the superlative value of a man who is able to express his emotions towards the woman he loves. As a man with a measure of discernment, I am neither afraid nor ashamed to express my emotions towards the woman I would want to love, and the next few pages will help you to understand the reasons why. I freely give the woman of my choice ownership to explore the depths of my soul. Every expression in this book, both individually and collectively, reflects my message that a man should exclusively love, honor, and treat with the utmost respect the woman in his life.

In what may be considered as unorthodox, I am extending an invitation for you to regard yourself as my woman of choice. I am sending forth my love as if on wings of angels, to reach out and inspire you no matter where you may be. Please accept my invitation, and allow me to caress the feelings of your heart with my tender affections of love. Open your heart, please, to receive intimacy on a level that you have always desired to feel from a man. Yes, intimate expressions of thoughts from the heart of a man in terms that you can relate to as a woman.

By accepting my invitation, I will use love in a poetic way to influence you to tear down your walls of ill-conceived ideas of love about a man. I will help you to rebuild your foundation with him so that both of you can find ecstasy in your love. In ways that you have not considered, I will use my knowledge of love to build you up and inspire you to keep your hope in love alive. I will restore your confidence in a man's ability to express his love as I soothe away the anger, the bitterness, and the disappointment from your heart. If you allow me, I will teach you how to use better judgment to redefine your present definition of what a man's love should be. If you allow me, I will teach you what is the most important thing that you must learn about a man that will endear him to want to give to you freely all the possessions within his heart.

I humbly submit to you that not all men's hearts are able to express their feelings in the way that a woman would like, although this fact in itself does not necessarily take away from the character of the man. However, as a woman, you still need to hear words of love and encouragement from time to time. So, I also invite you to allow my voice to serve as the spokesman of your loved one as you read through the pages of this book. By accepting my invitation, it will also give me an opportunity to speak to you in an indirect way that will show my appreciation for all the contributions that you bring to life. May I suggest that we meet at a time and place that are free from distraction?

I have many things that I would like to share with you, but the time that we spend together is totally at your discretion. Your feelings are very important to me, so I would like to encourage you to personalize this book by writing down your thoughts as you read the poetry and letters. Perhaps one day we will meet, and just think of the conversations that we can have! If we never do meet, it is my wish that, each time you read a portion of this book, I can remind you in some small manner how a man's love for his woman should feel. Whenever you need to hear words of love and encouragement, remember that I will always be just a page away. Now come with me as I share with you all the emotions that other men yearn to say, but cannot. Come with me, as I take you on a journey that begins at the center of a man's heart.

Author's Note:
If you read the invitation by following the directions on the back of the cover, please take time to read the preface now before you continue.

Revealing the Man of Love™

It is my belief that the highest compliment a woman can bestow upon a man is to consider him a Man of Love™. I am speaking to you in a womanly sense. I am speaking of a man who envelops you with a loyal love that is intense, pure, clean, and able to reside so deep  within your inner parts that you cannot distinguish him from yourself. I am speaking about the characteristics of a man who has so much substance that no amount of fear within you can withstand the nature of his love. With words unspoken, the quality of his love commands your deepest respect.

I imagine this form of communication with a man may seem unrealistic to you in view of our times, since a woman's hope of finding true love usually never materializes. There are various reasons for this, but usually the signs of failure are traceable to the selection process. I will not pretend to subscribe to the illusion that a man selects the woman of his choice, while it is very commonplace for a woman to extend her love unselfishly towards the man of her own choosing. Unfortunately, the end commonly results in the rejection of her love by him, thus leaving her emotionally scarred when the realization of his "I love you" rings hollow, and the meaning of his words equates only to having sex. Across different cultures and nationalities, the voices of women respecting their men are unified in saying:

"I want you as my man to be faithful to me. I want you to provide for me and show appreciation for the work that I do. I want you to engage me in conversation, instruct me spiritually and be concerned about my emotional welfare, by embracing me within the strength and security of your arms. I want you as my man to express your love for me physically, after attending to these other things first. Then my love will flow like cascading waterfalls, whose gentle waters will lead you out into the sea of my love, where no man has ever been able to explore its depths."

If your feelings are similar, or you can just simply relate to these words, then allow me to restore your confidence in love. Your Man of Love™ does indeed exist. He wants so very much to be a part of your life, if you will allow him to love you. He is simply waiting on you to recognize him. Throughout the pages of this book, I plan to reveal to you, in the first person, the qualities that define the Man of Love™ and the characteristics that his love displays. The love that I will be presenting to you is by no means blind, gullible, naïve, or to be compared to a teenager's infatuation. Rather, its intention is to show you a surpassing way of love, through various expressions of poems, essays, and letters that uniquely explain from my eyes, how this love should relate to you.

In defining the Man of Love™, from what source shall I draw my authority? It's been proven on many occasions that the conventional wisdom of those who speak from their own originality have no stability, and any success is short-lived at best. I am, however, relying upon the guidance of the Supreme Authority on love—God himself, because God *is* the epitome of love! Furthermore, in considering that man will never know all there is to know about Him, it is only logical to deduce that we will never know all there is to know about love. However, by pursuing and applying His knowledge, we can be confident that there will never be a shortage in our ability to both broaden our view of love, and to always express it properly. When man was created in God's image, he was endowed with a measure of God's four attributes—love, power, wisdom, and justice—love being the predominate quality that brings balance to the other three. As a man who seeks the guidance of the Universal Sovereign, how will my thoughts of love affect you personally as a woman? I believe that you will benefit as my voice guides you through the various emotions of a man that will encourage you and remind you how love should feel. By using a fraction of love's restorative powers, I can build you up with reminders of how special you are to life and instill within you that you do make a difference in the grand scheme of things. From this point onward, I am assuming my role as the spokesman of a man desiring to love you. Right now, if I were physically in your presence, I would treasure our time together, in that I would honor you by not wasting precious moments debating elementary principles of love; that leads only to contention. Nor would I succumb to adolescent behavior and put your love for me to the test. Rather, my starting point with you is to enter your love with maturity, as a full-grown man with understanding in its ways, in order to converse with you about the deeper and more significant aspects of love.

First upon entering, let me say that love is manly. Yes, love is manly in every sense of the word, because love is not just a feeling possessed by women; rather, love originates from a male Creator. Every conceived expression of love by us is nothing more than an imitation of what He has already done. I embrace the qualities of His attributes, and I concede to their value, so that I can love you as a man with complete competence. For the power of love is a reckoning force of masculinity that draws you to me, and the effects of it within move me to act with you in a positive way. Love compels me to treat you with compassion. It compels me to be affectionate with you and openly use terms of endearment. Love tempers my authority over you and allows the usage of my power only as a last resort to bring about reconciliation. The spirit of love allows me to separate you as a woman from your behavior, and, by using wisdom, I can readjust you lovingly in its ways, if necessary, in order to preserve our union. In all of its glory, love never makes me feel ashamed of displaying proper affection for you in public; nor am I afraid of the consensus of those that may view my affection for you as a contemptible weakness. For if any outside action proves hostile or comes as an assault upon us, rest assured that I am a warrior for justice. I will declare war with the same intensity as my love for you.

❄ cont.

Although love is often construed as being a romantic or a sought-after "feeling," I believe love encompasses much more, because the many facets of it go beyond mere intimacy. Love is a driving force that provides comfort for the depressed; it strengthens the weak, it fights for justice, and it binds the family arrangement with bedrock principles. There is, however, one aspect of love that affects you more profoundly than others do. I have uncovered that there are no laws that limit a man from showing too much love, kindness, and affection to his woman. Although an essential Bible principle is that "A man should love his wife as he loves himself," I take the position to further this mandate and say: "I will treat you *better* than I treat myself." This is *my* standard! This is my definitive line of excellence that I have drawn, in order that you may firmly believe in my desire to love you with a complete heart and to keep the very existence of my love alive within you, no matter where you may be. For I believe that, within you, there is an enormous ability to love, and across great distances, we are able to share the same heart.

Through my poems, essays, and letters, I want you to indulge in the fullness of my love. Please accept it, by sharing your feelings with me in the spaces that I have provided for you to express your thoughts. When you have written your thoughts with my words, at the conclusion of this book, we will have created a unique masterpiece—a masterpiece that cannot exist without your personal thoughts. This is just the beginning. Love is waiting for you throughout these pages. As we continue the journey, I have but one ultimate goal. My goal is that you will see the reflection of my love within yourself and conclude in your own time that I am worthy to receive the title as your Man of Love™. This is not an expectation that I imagine receiving from you overnight, but over time, as you come to intimately know my personality and convictions. Now that I have revealed myself to you, please come to me.

Come to Me

My love,

If you have grown tired of the relentless pursuit of love that has led your heart into despair; if you have grown tired of measuring a man by his stature, and you are ready to look at the thoughts and intentions of his heart, then come to me and let me refresh you. For your ears will  never hear abusive words from me. Your eyes will never bring forth tears out of sadness. Your heart will never become faint out of fear, because I am willing to accept you with all of your imperfections. Come, let us talk intimately with each other. You can come to me without a deceptive heart and speak freely to me without feeling ashamed. For I am not here to judge you. I am here to offer you a love tender in affection and with enough excitement to take you beyond your expectations!*

Accept my love, and I will refuse to define the boundaries of my love for you by special calendar events created by someone else. Instead, I will lead the way to redefine the depths as to how a man should love his woman. I will set a new standard—one that man has not known. In doing so, may God declare that "Never has a man loved a woman like I have loved you." In considering that my display of love for you extends beyond His mandate, may God decide that it would be unrighteous to allow one of us to remain to mourn the loss of the other. May He answer my prayer for us to expire together and be reunited into a world where death can never, ever pose a threat and come between us again. Into eternity, I want to continue to love you to the glory of Him who gave me the ability to love you. So come to me. This love is reserved for you. I am waiting for your arrival, patiently.

I have prepared my heart for you. Indulge.
Taste, and enjoy my love.

Please share how you are feeling at this moment:

My love is a way of life.
Rendezvous with me in paradise.

I.

THE QUEST FOR LOVE

Real Love Exists—in the Most Unlikely Person

I was a stranger to you, someone you thought did not exist. Open your heart, please, and allow me to take you to a place of beauty where I can nourish you with inspiration. If, through my poetry, you can hear the softness of my voice speaking to you, and if you can feel my intensity as a heartbeat, then breathe life into me, and let me enter into your passion.

Deep within, you have always known me
I am the man's face in your dreams, but never revealed
Listen, my love
Your heart knows the sound of my voice
I have come for you
With tender affection to conquer your fears
In faithfulness to instill your trust
I am the dream
Surrender your heart to me

For your breath gives me life as if a new force of energy
All that I can become begins and ends with you
It is you who can make our lives complete
Now that I have opened my soul
Hold on to me so I won't fade away
For I fear I may never find my way back to you

Listen. Listen intently to me, my love
I have come here just for you
With a willing heart to show you a life of love
If your heart is willing to surrender to my love

I'm listening. Share your feelings:

_____

_____

_____

_____

_____

_____

_____

_____

_____

_____

_____

_____

_____

_____

_____

_____

_____

_____

_____

_____

_____

_____

_____

_____

_____

_____

_____

_____

_____

_____

How do I tell you that you're beautiful, without coming on too strong?
If my heart reveals what I feel, I may scare you away
So if I stutter or say the wrong things, it's only because I'm nervous
For you make my mind swirl in a maze and
Looking at you simply takes my breath away
There are so many things I want to say, but
Where do I begin with only one impression to make?
I look for a sign that welcomes me to advance
The countdown begins, and in 30 seconds it's too late
You turn away, and in my silence I yearn for you to stay
Yet, I remain silently in love with the image of a woman
That a man often dreams of

In my silence, I look at you when you can't see me
Wondering if you believe in falling in love
I imagine, in an instant of time, you understanding that
I want to be the strength your heart is searching for
To make you feel like the woman you are
I want to know the moisture from the softness of your lips
Feel the curvature of your hips
Explore the natural wonders that only you can give
I am intense
I am afraid
Release me with your smile
As I stand at a distance in awe of your beauty
Set me free from your silent love
For you are the image of a woman that a man dreams of

To my silent love,

I do not even know your name, but the memory of you will haunt me forever. For one brief moment, your eyes told me that paradise awaited me. In that moment, I became a living statue and doubted myself. I do not know why or how I let you simply walk away. In that instant, I became the greatest of all fools for not exploring our conversation further. Rightly so, I take my place in the hall of shame. In my moment of hesitation, I lost more than the opportunity to experience the tenderness of your affection. Now I must mourn the loss of your companionship.

For me to say that my heart is only saddened to know that I may never deserve to meet you again is an understatement, since I will never be able to find redemption without divine intervention. For without it, what are the chances of us meeting again? Now I must live with the error of my hesitation in knowing that you will find love in the arms of another man. If, by divine intervention, we could ever meet again, know that I would confess my intentions to love you with a oneness of mind. With joy in my heart and humility in hand, I would tell you that it was I who failed you. It was I that failed us; but never again would I allow fear to keep me from pursuing the love that I saw within your eyes.

So, if you should ever read this, know that my love is waiting to reclaim our lost moment in time. Wherever you are, send me word that you are free, and I will meet you in the valley of your paradise. I will travel great distances to be with you, because I would rather live in a foreign land with you than live a life of solitude in my homeland without you. I know that second chances in love are only given to a select few in life. I am asking you to give us a second chance to know the love that we should have known the first time. I promise you that I will not make the same mistake again.

The face of love changes with time
It was much different when you were younger, yet
You yearn for it as you continue to search for "the feeling"
"The feeling"—in whom your heart has put its trust
That has abandoned you to empty and meaningless relationships
Whose betrayal has left your heart to wander
To question if there is such a thing called love

But the love that you are looking for is waiting on you
It's waiting for you to come to maturity
Love is more than just the image of a man
It is more than just his spoken words
It's the experience over time that reveals his spirit!
Where the strength of his character is no longer a mystery
Love awakens you to realize that "the feeling" is your shared history
The feeling is a time of reflection

When he speaks, his words have meaning
He errs, yet makes amends, and forgiveness he freely extends
His love is without expectation—he receives no prize
A confidant you can trust—no deceit, no lies
He anticipates your arrival
As protector, as lover, as a servant to you
Bending to your wishes, yet firm in his convictions

He supports you to be the woman that you desire
While telling you his secret passions so that you
Can be the only woman that he desires

Above all, he takes time to ask
What do you like?
How do you feel?
What do you think?

So come, my love, and consider the unlikely
Consider more than the black and the white
Love is an array of colors! It's multifaceted!
Because there is more than one way to express it
Open your eyes and see the man of color
Yes, love is waiting on you
It's waiting for you to come to maturity

I am waiting to hear your thoughts:

I know other men have hurt you and let you down
And it's easy for you to say that all men are the same
I know it's hard for you to believe that there still exists a man
Who's willing to understand, comfort, and provide for you, but
Baby, here I am
The man you've been searching for

I know how it feels to want to give up on love
To think of it as a fantasy
I know how it feels to give your love to someone and
To have them turn you away
Make you feel lonely—insecure
Make you feel that life should come to an end, but
Baby, here I am
A man willing to risk injury to his heart

For I want to believe and put faith in you
Teach you how to love again through
The softness of my love
My time
My tender affection
My sole devotion that belongs to you
The softness of my love has no end
But it begins with the thought of you

Describe different ways in which I can be soft with you:

A best friend is what I want to be
To see life through your eyes
And know that what you feel is real
I am expecting nothing from you as
I am giving you a willing heart
That will laugh, and cry, and sing, and love
To such a beautiful woman it can become
Your soul mate—the one you can freely love

Search, if you will, within this heart of mine
But you already know me
I am the feeling that you know but cannot describe
I am real
I am waiting here for you

To hold you in my arms when you need to be reassured
That everything will be all right
To wipe away with tenderness your tears
To comfort you and quiet your fears
I will always be there for you with

One voice
One heart
One mind

A best friend for all times

Describe how our friendship can be:

I have a secret
It is a dangerous secret for the woman who is unsure of her heart
If I tell you my secret, it will lead you to the fountain of my love
A treasure that only one woman can claim
Do you want to know my secret?

I will tell you my secret, but if you drink, you cannot turn back
You will not fully understand it, so you must drink with faith
Drink from my waters, and I will become a reflection of you
Like the image in the mirror penetrating to your very soul
Love me little, and your heart will always yearn to be loved
You must love me with trust
You must love me without fear
If you love me with every passion conceivable
I will enter inside of you with such intensity
That you will never feel the cold and need the warmth of a blanket
For l will consume you with such a burning desire
That it will fuel the flames that can never be quenched
Until passion itself knows passion, and I
Yes, I will call upon all the forces of the universe and
Openly declare that you are my woman
Where I am, you forever more will be, and

Our love story will always be told throughout eternity
Our names will be written amongst the stars
Into the heavens and down into the very depths of the sea
All creation will sing about the glory of our love
The love that was, that is, and that will always be inseparable, and

We will become a testament for what other lovers will aspire to be
Yes, I have a secret, but
It is not for the woman who is faint or unsteady of heart

Tell me your secret thoughts:

Defining the Man of Love™

Part One

From a distance, I have captured your heart with the spirit of my love. Although you cannot deny that my love is strong, and at times, it has overwhelmed your senses, being afraid has never felt so good to you. For my love keeps calling out your name, as the resistance of your heart slowly wanes by its desire to feel the thrust of my passion and to relinquish control of your emotions to me. For the day is drawing near when your love will find completion in me, and it will explode with ecstasy—*never ever* to be held hostage again! No, *never* to be abandoned, but set free to fall in love with a man who only wants to fall in love with you! This freedom I offer to you, as I ask you to take your first step and consider more than just my words.

I ask you to define my love based on the merits of my *heart's* condition. Yes, I want you to know what *motivates* my heart to love you! For I do not want you to just give your love away to the feelings of romance, but I want you to *invest* your love in the *qualities* of my figurative heart that is defined by my spirit. My spirit of *love, joy,* and *peace*. My spirit of *long-suffering, kindness,* and *goodness.* My spirit of *faith, mildness,* and *self-control.*

For these, my love, are the essential qualities that I must develop within me as a man in order to complete you as a woman. These qualities embody the values necessary to sustain our relationship during its infancy and well into maturity. My "love" by itself is not sufficient, because this one spirit alone cannot withstand against the effects of our imperfections and the influences of the world. For us to be successful in love requires each of my spirits to work in concert with the others, and it is only through this harmony that I can achieve a oneness with you, thus bringing the quality of my love for you closer to perfection.

Enter My World . . .

Peer into my inner soul, and allow the beauty of my spirit to over-shadow your heart. Once inside, you will come to know my spirit. You will call out to me, and I will answer you with the warmness of my kiss that will cause the melting of your heart. As you begin to slowly close your eyes, my passion will overwhelm you when I tenderly take your last breath away. At that moment, you will release one last sigh, as you feel the weakness of your knees and fall helplessly into the security of my arms that are cushioned with the softness of my love.

Each day thereafter, I will refresh you with waters as gentle as the morning dew, and you will unmistakably compare the beauty of my spirit with the sweetness of chocolate. I offer this to you with a willing heart. Do not be afraid to enter. Do not withhold your love from me, and there will be no goal that will be impossible for our love to achieve.

Observe His Spirit of Love

I am writing a story about you. It is a compelling love story that will reveal the answer to the ultimate question: "Why do I love you?" Although you have waited anxiously to hear me say, "I love you"—what your heart really wants to know is if my words have real meaning. Your heart, I have also discerned, is afraid, since you have sought to find a satisfactory answer to this question from men before me, and, because you desperately wanted to believe in them, you accepted less than the truth. Distracted by objects of affections that tarnish, break down, but that awed you at first sight, your heart was deceived into believing that this was proof of love. Yet in the end, you did not find contentment in them, and now that I have spoken the same words to you, you wonder what makes me any different. The difference is in my story.

My love story about you does not begin with extravagant fanfares or objects to win you over, but it speaks heart to heart with you. For at the core of my heart, I live my life by principles. In turn, my principles guide my love to try to do what is right and treat *all* people with respect. You, however, are a special exception in that I am willing to give you more of myself in terms of the amount of my tenderness and affection. I must warn you, however, that by doing so, I want your heart to fall in love with mine. This is the reason why, in each chapter of our lives, I will openly show you my heart, and the place where my love resides. There is no misdirection to make you believe that I am more than what I am. The more time we spend together, the more you will come to understand what the meaning of the word "love" means to me.

I breathe life into the words "I love you." It takes on a life of its own, so that the climax of my love story begins when I transfer that life to you. Through tender expressions, you will come to know my love intimately, as a man who shares your same values—a man with outpourings of emotions that can open sensations inside of you that you never thought could exist and excite those that lay lifelessly to reawaken themselves. In my love, you will have strong emotional outcries, as you cycle through many of your feelings in an attempt to sort them out. In time, you will come to trust my love, believe in my love, and you will call my love your best friend. For it is necessary for you to go through this cycle to differentiate that my love is not about the moment—it is about the spirit!

When you read deep within the heart of my story, my spirit of loving you releases your love from the oppression of fear. I set you free to explore within yourself and to soar beyond your own expectations. It is in my love that your love will find its salvation, because only with me will you find a continuous supply of everything that you will ever need! Although your beauty may attract me to you and your physique can lure me inside of your lair, I prefer to love the woman within your heart. My spirit knows that your heart is compatible with mine, and I offer you my "conditional" love simply because *I want to*. So how do you know this to be true? Just reflect on the ways that I have revealed myself to you, and let my manner of love serve as my witness.

In the time that you have known me, never have I placed any unreasonable demands on you, nor have you had to do anything to "earn" my love from me. You have known my love to be truthful—firm at times on matters of principle, yet yielding on lesser issues. I freely share my possessions, and I always ask you for your thoughts. I give my all to you in everything that I do, and, in return, what have I asked back from you? Nothing except that you love me faithfully and stand by me. For this is our covenant, and I have vowed that, as long as you do not break it, there will never be an ending to the story of my love for you.

Discern His Spirit of Joy

Would I die for you? I asked myself this question as I pondered over what the realization of my answer should mean. If, in my heart, I can truthfully say "no," then it does not necessarily mean that I do not have love for you, but it does reveal that something significant is missing between us. By admitting to this truth, it is a first step towards working on developing the type of bond that should exist between us as a man and a woman. I say this because, inherently, men have given their lives for their children, their beliefs, and even for less-than-honorable reasons. With the exception of God, I know of no nobility greater than a man willing to die for his woman's love. Therefore, after considering this question carefully, I can honestly answer "yes." I do so not out of expectation but for what my commitment to you means.

My commitment involves more than having only a sense of duty to-wards you, because my heart is already loyal in love to you in this life. The realization of saying "yes" means that I do not need to wait for death to show my appreciation for you in life. I reason that, if I would sacrifice my life for your love, then how much more so should I find pleasure in living for your love? That is why, every day, I observe the things surrounding me that remind me of you, and, within my heart, I purposely look for new reasons to rejoice in the comfort that your love provides. Nothing escapes my eye! I notice the small trinkets that amuse you and the slight change of your hairstyle. Even the missing earring does not elude my attention! For me, recognizing everything about you and paying attention to your subtle changes within, are always causes for celebration, because it keeps me connected with you on a level that is surreal. This surreal feeling is so overwhelming at times that you wonder what keeps me motivated to love you in this way.

I have come to realize that my love for you means nothing if it does not have joy. I take delight in the smallest of things that may not mean anything to others but is very important to me. It pleases me just to hear the sound of your voice. I delight in watching over you when you are sleeping, and I find contentment knowing that, when I lay my head down, you are asleep next to me. When I think of indulging in your fantasies, it is more than just excitement to me. It is like an epic adventure that I desire to navigate, so that I can understand the pleasure center of your mind. When I awake by the dawn's light with you in my arms, I find satisfaction in greeting you with a morning kiss. It is in these simplistic things that I live for your love, but the realization of my "yes" still goes much deeper.

I realize, too, that even when despair strikes at our hearts, it can take away the joy of living, but it does not take away my joy of wanting to be there for you in your time of need. Constant work is necessary for us to continue to grow in our love; however, I never think of the work involved in loving you as a form of drudgery. I view it as an enjoyment of living my life to the fullest! I find pleasure in planning a day of work, knowing that I am laboring for our love. I take pleasure in listening to your desires and planning for the realization of our dreams. I enjoy spending the time to plan surprises for you—just to see the expression of happiness on your face! I like being able to laugh with you and at the quirky things we both do in our imperfection. I like holding your hand and taking long walks with you, sharing our thoughts while dining together, and relishing every other imaginable idea that a man and a woman desire to do. In my mind, I would not hesitate to die for you, but I definitely would much rather live for you! In all that I have said to you, there is only one last thought that is missing. I want you to know that my joy of loving you is fulfilled when I wake up, and I am blessed to have one more day of life that I can share with you.

The Man of Love is Long-suffering and Kind

Invariably, imperfection will cause an adverse situation to occur that will affect the peace of our relationship. When this happens and you are in error, I face the delicate challenge of readjusting your thinking without condoning the behavior, but that will also result in reconciliation. To be successful requires that I use wisdom and focus my attention solely on the behavior in question without criticizing you. My success also depends on my level of empathy and my ability to accept that, with imperfection, a person receiving counsel for an error can sometimes find it difficult to embrace. If this happens in your case, then my challenge demands greater patience, as it may require an extended period for your wisdom to recognize that the behavior was not appropriate.

During this period of difficulty, I also recognize that I must manifest endurance with my patience. I must be kind to you in every respect by refraining from sarcastic remarks, the "I told you so" attitude, and the venting of my frustrations on you in terms of abusive speech. In no way do I want to withhold my love as a sign of protest, even when there is little or no progress, and even when we may experience a setback. For this period will fully test my resolve, and it is my hope that my long-suffering and kindness will lead to the softening of your heart and will cause you to listen to my voice. However, even with my best efforts, I know that I still have to consider the possibility that you may never accept readjustment and that I may simply have to extend forgiveness and cover over your error.

Overlooking your error will not always be easy for me to do. However, being aware that some adversity is going to occur one day, I am going to do all within my power to make it as *easy* as possible for you to accept my counsel. By taking positive actions now, I can minimize the strain to our relationship later, because my best defense for tomorrow's dilemmas is to influence you with love today. Indeed, how I treat you today will set the trend as to how you will respond to me in the future. When I influence you with love, I am building, in effect, our relationship—with the only fire-resistant material that can withstand the most intense wildfires. It is only by influencing you with love that our relationship has a realistic chance of survival, because the influence of love consistently uses kindness, goodness, and mildness to reassure you that I truly have your best interest at heart.

My use of these qualities is a real demonstration of my affection, because *it is* within my abilities to use this power of influence to make it *easier* for you to accept my counsel or to follow my lead. It is within my power to influence you to heed my guidance when I make decisions that reflect a family-first attitude. It is also within my power to persuade you to listen to me by not carelessly trampling on or disregarding your feelings. Without question, it is within my power to affect you to be willing to discuss any issues by being the first to open the lines of communication and to be reasonable in settling matters quickly. For there is no greater source of direction than for me to lead by example, and my use of love as an influence will always win over any sort of manipulation or any type of aggression.

Influencing you with love does not mean that you will always agree with my direction, nor does it guarantee that you will always respond in a positive way. Nevertheless, I take this stance today to increase our chances of survival, because, eventually, our own imperfections and external forces will threaten the safety of our relationship. As a man who promised to love and protect you, I plan to reasonably do everything in my power to be ready for adversity whenever it should come.

The Man of Love Is Not Jealous, Boastful, or Prideful

The power of love is in its simplicity to allow *you* to say, "I want to." Those words are priceless when coming from your heart, and I can have extraordinary faith in them when I consider the depth of your love for me compared to your civility towards another man. In other words, I know that if you decide that you want me to have your heart, then it does not matter how good-looking another man is. Nor does it matter how much money, power, or social status another man has, because I have nothing to fear from him. The fact that another man may covet you is only an indication that he is envious of me. I will not dignify covetousness with senselessness and devalue the meaning of a diamond heart that already belongs to me.

Although I have possession of your heart, I am not foolish enough to believe that the *possibility* of you never leaving me does not exist; however, I am more concerned with eliminating the *probability* of you doing so. If I treat you with dignity and respect, as well as show appreciation for the value that you bring into my life, then I have every reason to be secure and confident of your love for me. On the other hand, if I were to allow a place for jealousy and channel my positive energy into being overly suspicious and possessive without just cause, then I would become an imbecile. I would prove that I am unworthy of your love. Therefore, my mind is not preoccupied with the longings of another man. I am more concerned with myself and in how I can form perimeters of love that will protect the initial confidence you placed in me.

By protecting our hearts with heavily guarded boundaries, I can fortify your love for me within each perimeter, because our boundaries allow us freedom of choice; yet, it provides limits that preserve the integrity of our union. As a couple, neither one of us should be so confined that it will not allow for personal growth and creativity. With the inclusion of our Creator and heeding the adoption of His moral principles, we will always have the perfect set of boundaries that we can trust and that will always prove beneficial. Our imperfections, however, can cause rifts in our stability, but it is still possible to safeguard against even our own imperfections that are divisive in nature.

While it is normal to expect to face the enemy on the outside of our perimeter, there can develop a more dangerous and insidious enemy on the inside. If I am not careful, my self-reliance can make me too self-assured, which can lead me into arrogance. I alone can do more damage on the inside of our perimeter than any other person can do on the outside. If I damage the core of you "wanting to" such that it is beyond repair, then my defense perimeters will implode. If I am not conscientious about my arrogance, it will lead me to lose my humility and cause me to think too much of myself. I will become a braggart and will elevate myself to a superior position over you at the expense of demeaning your character. My appreciation for you will fade, and the warmness of a heart that you once entrusted to me will turn cold, because I will have lost the quality which every man needs to succeed in love.

Every man must have humility to keep the perimeters impenetrable from the outside and from collapsing from within. For this very reason, I embrace my imperfections, as they serve as a constant reminder of my humanity. I am not self-made. My knowledge is not absolute. You contribute to my success, and I need you in my life. So, I am mindful not to think more of myself than I should, because no matter what great accomplishments I may have achieved, at the end of each day, I am still nothing more than just a man—a man whose strengths in talents and abilities must always be used to benefit you and to provide refreshment for our relationship.

A Moment for Reflection

- What are the nine qualities that will reveal my true feelings for you?
- When you examine me, why is my love, by itself, not enough?
- Do you really know *why* I love you, and what my love stands for?
- How does my joy relate to my love for you?
- Why should you be able to see the quality of long-suffering in me?
- Why is kindness a vital part of being long-suffering?
- How can you make it *easier* for me to be long-suffering towards you?
- If my love for you were on trial, what would you say to convince the jury that my love is more than just a "feeling" of passion?

WILL YOU CONSIDER MY FEELINGS?

Are you concerned about how I feel as a man? If so, how do you think I might feel and react if you ...

    a. reflect a spirit of male resistance towards me?

    b. will not fully support me in my decisions?

    c. readily embrace counsel from others but scrutinize mine?

    d. believe that your love is irreplaceable and take me for granted?

    e. use manipulation tactics rather than influencing me with love?

    f. have a tendency to be overly possessive?

    g. consistently find fault with me?

Inside Your Heart

- How would you describe how you feel at this point?

- If you feel that you can trust my love, I will take you any place that you would like to go. Where should we go? How long do you want to stay there?

- Would you like me to kiss you? If so, where would you like me to kiss you?

- What song would you like to hear playing in the background when I kiss you?

- How do you think I feel about you as a woman?

A Suggestion of Love

Before reading my last thoughts in this chapter, if you are not already in a comfortable area that is without any distractions, please find a place where we can be alone. I would like you to light a candle for me, so that, in a symbolic way, my words can find their way to the deepest parts of your heart. Before you turn the page, relax your mind. I want to fill your heart with inspiration by sharing two separate thoughts that I feel are equally important; yet, they complement each other as a means of showing you how a man feels when he loves his woman. I pass my inspiration on to you!

❋ cont.

The beauty of a rose is in its petals. Although the rose has thorns, the thorns serve to protect the petals.

Caring for My Rose

With the pleasant scent of baby's breath, I will arrange our love. With gentle hands, I will caress your delicate petals. With tenderness, I will prepare your bed until you flourish each spring. Come to know me. Give me your support. Trust in my abilities, and I will protect you.

A Woman's Power

My love,

Wherever you are, hear my voice; listen intently to me. I am speaking to you from deep within. My voice exists at this moment for the sole reason of reminding you of the value that you bring to life. You are woman. You are a woman of immense power. Your feelings are the source of your strength—feelings that are instinctive by nature. Your instinct, combined with the power to reason, gives you an edge. Your power is quiet in nature, compassionate, and when used with respect, can make a man acknowledge it on a bended knee. You are woman.

These are not just words on a printed page. Feel them the way that only a woman can feel, and recall that your power has been alive from long ago. How many battles have men fought for a woman's honor? Have not men given up kingdoms for the love of a woman? Did not the angels forsake their dwelling places in the heavens to know the beauty of your love? Did not a man, to the detriment of us all, choose his woman over his God? I remind you—that You Are Woman.

Now rise, and go pursue your dreams. Realize your potential, knowing that emotionally, I will provide. You know me to be a man who is well refined and that I am not intimidated by your success; wealth and material possessions do not define me, and you also know that I am very passionate about you. With a fiery zeal, I will not just give you my attention, but I will place all of my resources at your disposal to ensure your success. So I say to you once again, that, You...Are...Woman. At this moment, you are not just any woman—You Are My Woman! For whatever glory you receive only adds to my own brilliance. You know my words to be true—now rise. Embrace your power, and know it...as only a woman can!

Love
Joy
Peace
Long-suffering
Kindness
Goodness
Faith
Mildness
Self-control

Will you judge me by my appearance alone? Look inwardly, and see the attributes of my mind and the qualities of my heart. Stop resising me. Open your heart and let my feelings flow ... **Passionately Within You!**

II.

LOVE CONQUERS

Capture His Mind—His Heart Will Follow

I hear the cry of despair in your heart that is being held in captivity. I hear the song of all the fallen men that lie before you. Capture my mind, and I will unleash the fury of my passion that will subdue in the midst of your fears until I penetrate to the chamber of your innermost walls. It is there that I will make my last stand to secure your love.

Unlike the fallen men, I will prevail, for I will not wield my sword towards your last protector. Nor will I try to conquer your defense apart from you. Before your eyes, I will draw my strength from the source of your love, and, with all of my might, I will prove myself as the only man worthy enough to harness its power. With the invincibility of a knight, I will enter within your heart. With the softness of my kiss, I will release its power inside of you.

I wish that I could be everything that you always wanted in a man
The kind who has just the right looks
The kind who always knows the right things to say
But I can only be who I am, so I need for you to give me time
So that I can show you that my words have meaning and
In return, I will give you the gift of love
That comes with a promise

I promise that I will never lie to you or seek the love of another woman
For I do not need to go back into the land of Egypt to realize
That you are the manna that I need to sustain me
I view you as a blessing from God and
I will not take you for granted
So I intend to marry you and taste love flowing with milk and honey
Bathing only in waters with your scent
Being content with a love that is righteous and pure

You feel so soft, and, baby, you smell so sweet
Come closer, and let me hold you in my arms
As I confirm my love for you, because
I can see in your eyes that you want to believe in me,
But you are so afraid—afraid that this isn't real

Yet the tears of your loneliness have been favorably heard, and,
Out of heaven itself, the spirit of love has descended upon me
To shower you with affection, and
With all my heart, my love believes in you
Hopes in you, and will endure all things to come

I am way past the bloom of youth and
I am willing to lose myself in you
To explore deep inside your riches
I want to live the dream with you
Kiss me and lose yourself in me

What would the dream be like for you?

I still find it hard to believe that you're all the woman that I need
At first, I was afraid to give in to the feeling
I wanted to deny that this was happening to me
But your love was so strong that it overpowered me
It made me feel weak, yet it brought me joy
And I surrendered to your passion
I surrendered to the feeling of your love

I can't imagine going back to being all alone
I want to commit to you
I want to make a life with you
You are my woman, and I want to be with you

The feeling of your love elevates me to a new high
It's crazy
It's absolutely wonderful
And it's so sensible for me to say
I love you

Describe how your love feels:

Serenity is a place that I have prepared for you in my heart
The journey to Serenity is filled with laughter and adventure
There is plenty of romance, tears of joy, and the sound of children
It's Jah supported and Jah inspired
Serenity is a place that you can always call home

In Serenity...

My touch is more than just a touch ...
It's an exchange of our hearts
My kiss is more than just a kiss ...
It opens the door to the depth of your love
It takes me to the center of your universe
I know your thoughts, your feelings and emotions
As though they were my very own
I know the very essence of you
There are no barriers, for you are totally free
Free to express your love, to sing, to shout
Free to be the woman that you are

I am your watchman, whose decisions serve to provide protection
I am your knight, who defends and preserves our way of life
I am your king, whose only command is that you love me from within
But, foremost,
I am your steward, who asks only that you allow me to love you
And give my heart a home

Express how my serenity makes you feel:

How sweet your affection was to me
Into your bosom you brought me
Sharing your intimate affairs
Well along into the night
I grew to love your sincerity
The very foundation of your beauty
Oh, how I yearn to be embraced
By the warmth of your heart
Hear the whispers of your tender compassions
Acquiesce to a love without fear

In my quieter moments, I can still hear
The sound of your laughter and
The funny things you would say
But, most of all, I will always remember
When you loved me ... without fear

What intimate thoughts would you share with me?

Baby, I need to talk to you
Times are changing, and the days are going by so fast
It's so uncertain what is going to happen to us
So I stopped for a moment, and I looked into our future
I saw me committing my life to you before family and friends
But, before I came to you, I prayed on my knees
I poured out my soul from the depths of my heart
With tears, I cried out to my Father how much I loved you
I pleaded for the strength to ask for your hand
I asked for the needed courage
I asked for the needed humility
To lead our family in His wisdom

When I looked into our future
I saw us eating the pages of His word
Yet, I saw faces—lurking in the shadows
The changing faces of those who wanted to destroy us
But, as we ate, we became beacons of light
Shining ever so brightly
Shining upon the shadows with the brilliance of our love

When I looked into our future
I saw only goodness, beauty, and laughter
But what I remember the most was the feeling
The feeling that we were truly happy
We were truly satisfied with each other
Baby, this beautiful future awaits us
Will you marry me?

How would you envision our life together?

Defining the Man of Love™

Part Two

From the beginning, I opened my heart to receive yours. I have not withheld myself from you, nor have you found deception in me. When you look into the mirror, it now reflects my image, because we have become kindred spirits in love. On the day that we celebrated our love, I drew your bath water. Under candle light, with the soft, distinct sound of music playing, I gently brushed your hair as you relaxed in the aroma of waters filled with lanolin and soft scents of perfumes. I spoke to you in an undertone and eased the tension in your heart with laughter, preparing you that I may enter what I will always consider a holy place.

You invited me to come inside, and the symmetry of my love for you formed itself from every precious gem imaginable. It beamed forth with splendor, casting its radiance on all of your shadows. In the midst of its brilliance, you gained insight, as I laid a path of rose petals that your bare feet should walk upon, in order to lead you to the creation and the evolution of my love for you. When you reached your apex, my love transformed itself into a flawless, diamond-shaped heart that had a special inscription etched on it. Upon reading the inscription, you became fearful, and I reassured you that the inscription was true. Then I placed the diamond-shaped heart into your hands for safekeeping. You became fearful again, and this time I reassured you with a gentle kiss and told you as I looked into your eyes:

> *It is no longer necessary for me to hold on to my love. The splendor of my love is alive and exerts power, and other women can now see that it resides with you! For you are no longer just any woman—you are a woman dearly loved by me! Come journey with me, and let us escape the bonds of an ordinary love so that we can relish in the exquisite beauty of love's perfection.*

Perfecting Our Love

We knew our love could be perfected, but we did not know how. So we walked through gardens and smelled the fragrance of love. We danced in the midst of passion itself and were not singed by its fire. We watched in silence, high upon a mountainous terrain, as the sun rose above the horizon. We played in waters on sandy beaches, walking hand in hand until the sun set below the sea; but still our love had not reached its end. There  was something missing. There was something more significant to obtain.

It was not until the knowledge of love opened our eyes that we realized that perfect love casts off all fears. We began to understand the journey itself and that love has the potential to reach a level of spiritual comprehension far beyond mere intimacy.

So, unafraid, we made passionate love under the moonlight. Your cries of ecstasy were heard by the stars, as they gathered to witness your love shedding forth its tears, when the beauty of our spirits merged into one consciousness—breaching the boundaries of our imperfections and transforming the very essence of our love into a new life. Within the warmth of this love, we lay exhausted. We lay embraced in each other's arms as we drifted off to sleep. Yet, we were unaware that we would have to face a new time of testing before we could reach our final destination.

Understand His Spirit of Peace

Allow me to enter your heart, and I will not raise a strong hand of tyranny against your soul or force you to subject yourself to me. With knowledge and flexibility as my strength, I will willingly acquire from you *all* the possessions within your heart. For my love will transform itself into a listener to achieve peace with your soul, and it will also speak its mind to settle your disquieting thoughts. I will bridge our differences and reconcile them with reasonableness and with fairness. With humility upon my forehead, I will disarm your defenses with the golden words of "I'm sorry," "I made a mistake," and "I do not know the answer."

As my victory, I will mount my flag of authority within the fortress of your heart and claim you exclusively mine. For under the authority of my love, we will reside in peace. There is no need for shouting, anger, or abusive speech. The law of my love is simply to be more understanding, to forgive freely, and show mutual respect. As I am at peace with myself, I can take the lead in this respect and extend it to you, because enjoying a peaceful relationship starts with having contentment from within.

Within me, I have a balance that is not overly concerned with my own importance. In being myself, I do not need to prove that I am more than what I am or the best in the world. I am content with self-improving my own deficiencies and working in harmony with yours to build a sanctuary that we both can call home. I just want to be me, and I simply know best how to be me. You have come to know how I love, and you know the feelings of my joy. So come and experience the tranquility of my peace! As we lie embraced, knowing that nothing lies between us, let us celebrate our love with the nakedness that belongs to freedom.

Comprehend His Spirit of Long-suffering

I love you so much. You are the only woman I have ever loved and felt that I wanted to build my future with. We came together with one mind to live a way of life with principles and boundaries agreeable to our hearts. With the breeze of the wind blowing through your hair, you freely roam in the openness of my heart, like a stallion prancing with beauty and grace. Released from despair, your creativity abounds, and the scent of your love lingers in the air—enticing and seducing me, to return to love the only woman in my Garden of Eden. With the freedom that you possess, you must, my love, always be on guard against serpent-like influences who will covertly cause you to question our love. By using cleverly crafted reasoning, their aim is to cause divisions between us and to deceive you to go outside of your boundary lines.

As much as I love you, I cannot act unwisely and allow you to cross the border to run wild and unrestrained without a spoken word of dissent. If I did not contest, then I really would hate you more than my confession of love for you, because a breach of our principles always represents a threat to love. Ignoring any breaches only undermines our foundation and exposes our love to infectious viruses that are capable of destroying us. Also, if I simply did nothing to quash your seeds of doubts, in the end, your respect for me would erode further, and that as well would destroy us. So please, keep watch for the serpent's influences, because although my love for you is very strong, it cannot act indefinitely towards you, if, you persist in doing what you know is wrong.

As much as I love you, I will always maintain respect for myself. Although my love for you can be endless, my long-suffering has its limits, if you refuse to respond favorably. It is important that you understand that my long-suffering has a definite purpose concerning you. It means more than just enduring any pain or trouble that arises. Its purpose is to look after your welfare and preserve our bond of union. Its purpose is to safeguard our way of loving one another by seeking to reconcile wrong to right, which causes me to deliberately restrain myself from acting with haste. When I am exercising patience with you, I am also enduring as a means to counter the serpent's influence. By purposely restraining myself, I am essentially pleading for you to recognize the machinations of our enemy before it is too late. Keep in mind that, although the face of our enemy may change over time, his purpose is always the same.

Our enemy wants to destroy our love. Looming in the shadows, he waits to introduce thoughts and ideas contrary to the natural order of things in order to have us become discontent and feel as though we are depriving ourselves. He wants us to think only about ourselves and believe the structure of our family arrangement is an injustice. He even wants me to view being patient with you as a burden so that I may get discouraged and leave you, no matter the cost. However discouraged I may feel, rest assured that I will not give up so easily on you! Nor will I give in so easily to the tactics of our enemy! I know his ways, and I will fight against him, using the influences of love in order to save our love. To counter his effects, I am adopting an attitude of joy with my long-suffering. Why joy? Because joy is a positive attitude of love that can conquer any of his bad influences, and joy, is also the last emotion that he wants me to have towards you.

Therefore my love, if you ever get lost outside of your boundary, I will do my best to rescue you, by extending my hands to pull you back inside the safety of our love. Even though our love may not be perfect in every respect, our principles still serve as a protection for both of us. So run free, explore, and express yourself to your heart's content. Just remember always to take care to stay within the boundaries that were agreeable to both of our hearts.

The Man of Love Does Not Behave Indecently

Proof of love begins with common courtesy. For how could I ever form the words "I love you" if it were missing from me? Yet, you have never known it to be that way with me. My proof love is alive and proves itself—by the simplest of deeds—that you can clearly see is fulfilling its purpose within you. For like the brilliance of the sun, my love radiates from your heart—such that a glow is visible upon your face. With so much intensity, it causes all of your girlfriends to surround you, as they jealously ask of you the reasons why. Yet, in the heart of your heart, you always guard all of our secrets, as you constantly daydream and allow my love to consume your thoughts. For within your thoughts, you well know that I regard your feelings with the highest esteem and that my proof of love goes way beyond the occasional sending of a card or flowers to express my feelings for you.

My proof of love is evident each day, as I continue to pour into your heart an immeasurable amount of dignity, honor, and respect— such that your heart cannot always contain the overflow. For I have always shown you refined behavior—even when we have disagreed—and you have always received from me on the telephone, in private, and in public places, politeness and other well-mannered behavior. Never have you known with me the physical abuses that other women have had to endure. Never have you heard coming forth from my lips obscene language, nor has my conduct been grossly offensive to you. The manner in which I have chosen to love you throughout our relationship has always been based solely on the moral principles that govern my life.

My principles adhere to a high standard of conduct that will always be decent and courteous towards you, because I cannot even begin to imagine treating you any other way. Even when you do not fully appreciate the love that I extend to you, it is part of my nature to continue to be true to myself. For I believe that there will come upon you a day of enlightenment, in which you will reflect more profoundly on all the ways that I have shown you love. On that day of deep reflection, you will resolve that my love has proven itself to be more than just real. It will have proven itself to be like a fantasy that other women can only dream about in their lives. Your revelation will be the beginning of a celebration in which your love will finally find completion in mine, and, in your joy, you will feel compelled to tell your closest friends. It will prove to be so good in your eyes that your heart will want to bear witness about all of my ways in love. Although you may never tell me, or I may not be around when you tell others about me, you will complete the circle of our love when you can say affectionately from your heart regarding me:

> His *love* is in *everything*!
> It is more than just his touch!
> It means more than his kiss!
> I feel it when he says "please" and "thank you."
> I know it when he is at a distance away.
> He is a decent man.
> He is a gentle man.
> I can never be ashamed of him.
> All that he asks from my own hands, I cannot deny him.
> For he never takes more than what he needs.
> I could never give my love to any other man.
> I cannot imagine living my life without him.

The Man of Love Does Not Look for His Own Interest

Once in a lifetime, that someone special comes along, and you give all that you have. You do not think about yourself. You just love unselfishly from your heart. In time, that love becomes so beautiful that it is beyond describing, because it is not contrived, and there are no hidden designs. You are my once in a lifetime. All day long, I want to concern myself with you and become the only sentinel who looks after your welfare. I want to provide you with the comforts of life, with the security of knowing that my love is exclusively yours.

Many people say that when you are in love, you must compromise to get along. I suppose that there is a degree of comfort in accepting that statement—for those willing to settle for an ordinary love. I suppose that it makes it much easier for them to accept that their love can never find completion. However, this can *never* be acceptable to me! I will not accept defeat in the face of imperfection and concede that true love is an impossibility. I will not nurture our love and then simply forfeit it by holding on to a flawed reasoning that is imminent to fail. For I know that there exists a better way. Yes, there is a better way to bridge our love into the perfect bond of union.

The better way begins when I accept that I am not a servant to myself but to the commitment I made when I told you that "I love you." My commitment means that I seek to fulfill my own pleasures only *after* I have pursued first what is good in your eyes. My commitment means that, from the fruits of my own hands, I give you first choice. This is the better way, and it is my preferred way of loving you, because it is *never* a compromise in seeking your advantage. It is *never* a loss for me in fulfilling your desires. For I put my trust in believing that your love has the ability to rise above its own inclinations and that you will imitate me and love me unselfishly; creating a natural equalization between us.

It is this very bond of unselfishness that will shield us from accumulating hidden resentment in bartering for concessions or the unjust feelings of having denied ourselves simply to get along. This is the better way of love, and my preferred way of love can always be second, if it means that I will always be first in your affections.

Once in a lifetime, a man of conviction comes along, and his voice is not a stranger to your heart. I am that man. My voice is calling out to you, even now, to receive my love. For what I give to you is always free, and I always will give you more than what you need! You are the chosen one, because I hear the sound of only *your* voice echoing within my heart, and it has led me to my destiny. It has led me to you, and I have fallen in love.

The very joy of being with you is so intense that I cannot find the words at this moment to describe the beauty that I feel for you. I can only say that I have journeyed through the passion of love's desires, and I have refined everything that was good, and I have inscribed them in my heart to present them to you. For I want my love to reign supreme over any other would-be suitor's. With unspoken words, I want you to know me as the lord of your manor. I want to be the man to whom you can entrust your feelings, and for you to know me as someone who considers how you feel. I want you to know me as the man who is with you, the man who is for you. I want you to know that I loyally stand by you and that I am committed to the commitment of saying, "I love you."

A Moment for Reflection

- What do you think the inscription says that is written on my heart?
- During the transformation, what is the new life that came forth?
- What is our time of testing and our final destination?
- Can we learn to perfect our love? Explain.
- Why must perfect love have no fear?
- What will make it *easier* for you to subject yourself willingly to me?
- Why will the "golden words" maintain peace within our love?
- Why must our marriage have structure in order to have peace?
- Who are our enemies, and what type of masks might they wear?
- Why do you think "our enemies" want you to have...

    a. resentment towards my headship?
    b. feelings that submissiveness is an oppression that is degrading?
    c. a deep-seated hatred for the mistreatment of women?
    d. mistrust for me, such that you hide your material assets?

- How does the purpose of my long-suffering spirit affect you?
- What do you consider proof of my love for you?
- What is your proof of love for me?
- What is the better way for us to love each other?
- Why has compromising proven detrimental to relationships?
- Why will seeking your mate's advantage prove more beneficial?

- Are you concerned about how I feel as a man? If so, how do you think I might feel and react if you ...

    a. flagrantly display contempt for me?
    b. cringe at the mere thought of me having "authority" over you?
    c. show more respect to other people than you do for me?
    d. rarely or never offer me praise for the good things that I do?
    e. assert that I am trying to control you in order to have your way?
    f. mask your feelings, yet emotionally distance yourself from me?
    g. withhold your love as a means of coercion?

- Would you agree that you would like me to consider how you feel about the many challenges a woman has to face in her life? If so, then are you willing to view life from a man's point of view, so that you can understand my challenges, my frustrations, and the many obstacles that I have to overcome?

- Have you ever considered the psychological impact upon a man who *truly* strives to provide for his family but falls short because he:

    a. cannot make enough money to support his family?
    b. cannot find suitable employment due to valid reasons?

- Have you ever considered that I suffer in silence, because I do not know how to express my feelings as well as you do?

- Have you ever considered that my best is never good enough for you?

Inside Your Heart

- All that I have is yours. I will freely give to you the desires of your heart. If you close your eyes and make a wish, what would your wish be?

- I want to dance with you throughout the night. Will you dance with me? If so, what song would you select as "our song"?

- If I place the world in your hands and ask you to pick a place where we can celebrate our love, what place would you select?

- In what other ways can I show you more love and that will allow me to be more romantic with you?

Romancing Thoughts of Appreciation

I feel very honored that you have journeyed with me thus far. Taking time to reflect is very important in learning to appreciate the love a person has for you, just like there is great value in setting the right mood for an occasion. So, before you continue reading, please pour yourself a glass of wine or some other favorite beverage that you like. Please play "our song" that you have selected, and dance with me. I want to end this chapter with my appreciation for the often-overlooked contributions that you bring to life as a woman. Each portrait of love has value. Each thought has its own unique meaning that becomes a part of the sum total of who we are. You are indeed a reflection of beauty!

 cont.

Portraits of Our Love

A simple evening.

You looked so good in that black chiffon dress. Every detail about you was perfect. Dinner conversation was intriguing, and the performance affected both of us so deeply. It was a perfect evening. I *appreciated* the time it took you to get ready, the shopping needed to find just the right dress and the accessories to match. You wanted to look your best for me. Thank you.

A spontaneous day.

We played hooky from work and spent the afternoon playing in the park. You brought lunch in a basket. I fed you as we listened to music. I read you poetry, and you sang for me. We escaped reality for a day. I *appreciated* that you prepared food you knew that I would enjoy. The dinnerware was very nice, and I noticed the scented blanket that I could sit on and lay my head on. Overall, I *appreciated* the quality time we spent together.

Fun at sea.

Cruising was an adventure as we explored the islands. We tasted the native food on the islands and learned about their culture. We partied on the ship and spent time relaxing and spending time with each other. I *appreciated* that you planned this vacation and that you even over-packed for the trip! You wanted to make sure that we had everything so that our time together would be more enjoyable. I *appreciated* your thoughtfulness.

A special night we shared.

The weather was perfect. The breeze was refreshing as I watched the sunset with you in my arms. We talked intimately about all that was in your heart. Just as the sun was to go below the sea, you whispered to me that you wanted to fulfill a fantasy that had come to mind, and I, well, I was willing to please and was pleased. I *appreciated* the way that you openly shared your love with me!

What portrait of love comes to your mind, and what would you appreciate about it?

Your Love Song

In the beginning, I was all alone
Until the day that I heard your song ...

Your love song was so beautiful
Your love song was calling out to me
As I listened to the melody
There was something familiar about it
It was as if I had known it all of my life
I began to sing your song
I began to sing your song with so much passion

> With Joy
> With Love
> With Laughter
> With Tears

Because I knew the history of the words
I knew the arrangement of a lonely melody
In a thunderous chorus of voices
As we sang a duet that was familiar to no one else's ear
When we reached the crescendo, you came ...
You whispered that you loved me
My life has never been the same

Honoring Your Love

Your presence alone adds beauty to my world. When I reflect on the many ways that you extend your love to me, I realize that your love is more than just a feeling. Your love is like a fabric woven in every area of my life! You are deserving of praise for so many valid reasons. Although it is not possible for me to list every reason here, I do recognize that you are:

My loyal friend

My loving wife

My faithful lover

Your friendship has proven to be like the expansion of the sea. From the very depths of the ocean, your love has surfaced to caress me. You ascend above all other women that I have ever known, because your faithfulness is as reliable as the rising and the setting of the sun. May your glory live on to time indefinite. May I always be the receiver of your love.

A Woman of Wisdom

My love,

As one of the wise women, you have proven yourself to be just that. Your conduct gives testimony that you are indeed a woman worthy of praise. From your early days, you have understood that respect means as much to a man as love means to a woman. Although I cannot speak to the approval of our Creator, this is what I would say to Him concerning you:

"Jehovah, you created man in your image and crowned him with glory and splendor, and it was you, Jehovah, who gave him dominion throughout the earth. In your wisdom, You did not create woman separately from the man, but, with profound love and for the sake of the man, You created remarkable beauty out of him. It was Your will for woman's creation not to rival man's authority or to seek equality but to serve as a helper to him and to bring him to completion as a complement to him. By the works of her hands, woman would establish herself as the glory of man. By Your own divine authority, it was You, O Sovereign Lord, who arranged the union between man and woman and decreed that the two should act in harmony as one.

"Before you, Jehovah, I offer testimony to the character of the woman I have come to love, respect, and cherish. In my eyes, she has proven to be a God-fearing woman. Despite her imperfections and inclinations of the heart, she has struggled to maintain her virtue and integrity. An outstanding manifestation that her love for You is greater than it is for me is visible in the attitude she projects towards me. She views her submission to my headship as a greater respect to Your divine arrangement. She accepts her position as honorable and carries out her duties with grace and dignity. Jehovah, it is in your counsel that she has put her trust, despite the contrary advice from the inexperienced woman to

usurp my authority and rely upon her own strength to secure her future. Besides listening to Your counsel, there is further demonstration of her love for you.

"For my part, as You are well aware, I have tried to act responsibly towards her, but, with my own imperfections, I have not always listened to her opinion. On occasion, I have not acted in a manner deserving of respect. During those times of unfavorable conditions when she strongly disagreed with my position, she stated her objections, but it is noteworthy to mention that her conduct remained chaste and her speech pure. Even when I was persistent in making a colossal error in judgment, she willingly supported me in every way possible to try to make my decision succeed. In the face of defeat, her voice was reassuring, and my love for her increased tenfold when she told me that she still loved me and still respected my ability to make decisions. The fact that she restrains from showing sarcasm in her voice to me, indicates deep respect and empathy for my imperfection.

"I attribute her deep respect to the relationship that she has developed with You. In her quieter moments, she prays often on my behalf to You, and she petitions You to soften my heart to lend attention to her requests. Have you not, Jehovah, listened to her requests because of her fear of displeasing you? Have you not acted on her behalf and softened my heart? Have you not, Jehovah, interceded when I became unyielding and withheld from me my own requests until I treated her accordingly? Therefore, I bear witness that my wife is a woman worthy of praise. If I could go on, I would speak volumes about her additional qualities—from her modest but well-arranged dress to the hard work of caring for the family. I can find no fault with the manner in which she always conducts herself. I thank You for blessing me with such a capable and loving wife. She is priceless, and, because she relies upon You, I consider her a woman of wisdom."

No matter what lies ahead....
It was never a mistake to love you.

III.

A SEASON OF CHANGE

Mistakes Are Inevitable—They Perfect Love

In the beginning, our love was perfect. It was a glorious, short-lived moment of perfection. When the moment faded, we fell like stars from the heavens as familiarity set in and our imperfections became exposed. Behind your smiles were tears filled with fear, as we entered our darkest hour. Unknown to me was that my endurance of suffering in love would reveal its superlativeness to enable me to perfect it within myself to live a peaceable life with you in every season of change.

Now with eyes of understanding, future moments of perfection are only limited by our ability to embrace the lessons of our history. Disparaging moments are perfected with humility, kindness, forgiveness, and atonement. As we go through different phases of our lives, each moment presents unique opportunities for us to celebrate our love. Even though we cannot relive the past, our future is written by our present. As each moment passes, what we take away from the moment is what will define us. Love is progressive in its learning process, and it will refine our understanding. It will restore us, and it will lift us beyond our original hope in love.

I didn't realize ...
That I was destroying your dreams and expectations of me
I didn't understand ...
The depth of your love
I had no idea of how insensitive I was
Until I heard the echo of your love
Crying out to me

Just love me ... Just love me

I didn't realize...
That I caused the weakening of your love for me
With words so sharp, that cut so deeply
Spoken thoughtlessly ... all too naturally
Until I heard the echoes of your love
Lamenting its feelings for me

I loved you ... I loved you

Here I am, all alone
With the memories of a faded love
I have discovered my mistakes
I have learned how to listen,
How to pay attention and share outside of me, and yet ...
You don't love me anymore

Goodbye ... Goodbye

I admit that I have been wrong. How can I regain your love?

If I were to show you a tear
Would you think that I am less of a man
Or would you understand that I have feelings, too?
I can be sensitive to your needs
Because I want the same things that you want
For I'm just a man with a heart
Nothing more, nothing less

There will be moments when I will speak, but I won't listen
Fall short of giving you needed attention and
Selfishly put my needs before yours
But please,
Please don't turn away from me
I'm not perfect, and neither is my love
For I'm just a man with a heart
Nothing more, nothing less

Just a man with so many lonely nights
So much needed love
Just a man with so much love to give
So much emptiness within
I'm just a man with a heart
Nothing more, nothing less

How do you feel about me opening myself up to you?

Measuring My Love

How will you measure my love? When you tell the tale of our affairs, will it be a reflection of truth in love or a distorted view of missing facts, which makes a difference in perception? After all that we have shared, I want to know how you will measure my love for you. I know that, in times of good fortune, it will be very easy for you to define, but what about in the times of distress? I admit that I may not seem to be your everything in the wake of my imperfections; however, I know that I am more than just a man passing through your life. I am here to make a difference within you, because I still believe that I can be your everything. Although, at this very moment, you do not fully understand me, I have not given up on you. I am fulfilling the promise that I made to you, and this is my testimony of my commitment to that promise.

Inside my heart, I made the decision to love you in all seasons of your life; however, when I made that decision, it was not at the expense of becoming a "yes" man simply to please your ears. Admittedly, my love for you can always be improved upon, but, nonetheless, it is striving to be true to what it is. Its nature in intent is to learn from past and present feelings and combine them with desirable emotions to realize a better future with you. I do not know what measurement you will use to determine my worth, but my standard of love does come with integrity. It will never be for sale at any price, nor have I, or shall I, give it away haphazardly to any other woman. Within my circle of life, I chose you and with your acceptance, you agreed with me to nourish it that it may flourish to both our benefits. From our inception, you have always insisted upon truth and loyalty in the manner in which we love. One truth that you may not always want to recognize is that you have not always made it easy for me to love you, despite your claims of being a warm and caring person. This is relevant, because even if I fall short in your eyes, does that excuse you from being the woman you profess to be?

In truth, were you always the ideal woman when you spoke without thinking and used hurtful language? Did you ever consider that your snide and flippant remarks, which may have seemed amusing to say, were disrespectful to me? Did you communicate your feelings accurately with words that conveyed the correct meaning, or did you allow them to fester and explode unrestrained? Did you always represent a woman of integrity and virtue? Did you want love to come so easy that the thought of working hard at it mentally distressed you? Did you have more of an expectation of the man that you wanted me to be that you got lost in your own dream and could not accept me for who I really was? These questions do not require a response. I am only acting as a mirror for you to see the reflection of your own love. Have you truly proven to be the woman you profess to be, or will you use my short-comings as your perfect excuse for not becoming the woman of your choosing? I am not passing judgment on you; however, in weighing my love, what scale of truth will you use to balance my goods? Do you really want truth in our love?

Truth in love from an outside perception is a theme glorified in relation-ships; however, I truly say to you that, inside, it is seldom celebrated, be-cause truth highlights our individual imperfections that we are not always willing to accept. Thus, truth is often exchanged for half-truths, or dare I say, lies that are more palatable. What really is the truth be-tween us? Throughout our relationship, yes, I made tough decisions that were not always popular with you. I believed then, as I still do now, that, when certain principles are involved, a man must act accordingly and stand his ground with integrity, despite any backlash. My stance is not out of egotism but from my belief that, from the point of passively eating the forbidden fruit down to our day, it is evident that no man truly loves his woman by becoming a eunuch at her bidding, simply to gain favor. My loyalty in love to you also includes protecting you from yourself, as I stand guard at your temple to shield you from all other dangers. Under my watch, I have had to correct your misguided thoughts at times. Unfortunately, your defensive nature did not always receive my words as love, but, with an obstinate disposition, you rebelled against me and called it controlling and harsh criticism. Yet in truth, no amount of seasoning of words would have changed some of your preconceived attitudes. On some occasions, you stubbornly refused to listen to softer guidance, and certain words were needed to be said in order to get you to feel what you were not willing to hear. My intentions were never to hurt your feelings but to awaken your senses to the potential consequences of your thoughts or actions. If this is an error in my thinking, then charge it to my account, but at least credit me for good intentions of heart.

When you measure the quality of my love, will you consider the human fallacy of projecting our insecurities upon others? Out of our fears come misplaced indignation, false accusations, and even jealousy, creating inferiority complexes. From within your insecurities, you can easily mislabel my self-confidence as arrogance or find fault with me because of your inability to comprehend certain matters. Place on your measuring scale that any superior abilities that I have over you do not make me the better person. Our love is based on dependency, and my gifts in life are not in competition with you—they were given to me in order to complement you in areas where you might be weak, so that *together* we can stand strong. For this reason alone, I implore you not to allow your fears to destroy us.

In your final measurement, at what point will you find contentment in my imperfections and reconcile that, although we come from two different backgrounds, with different lessons in life, we do not have to be at odds? I advocate that we restore our faith and trust in our vow of dependency. I advocate that we return to love. Only you can determine the worth of my love, but I hope that, when you measure it, it is balanced and will reflect the truth in our love.

How do you measure a man's love?

Awaken

Long before my arrival in your life, you blindly gave your love away to men who were not ready to appreciate the precious value of it. You were so enthralled with wanting to be in love that you ignored the signs that told you to wait. The craving for male intimacy was so strong that you gave your best to men whom you barely knew. Yet, these men did not share your same value of love, and, in time, they eventually rejected and abandoned you. Now, because of those men's fatal mistakes, your perspective of love has changed for life, and you believe that their behavior represents all men. I say this to you because the time has come for you to awaken from this victimized way of thinking. It is time to reconcile your past, because it is affecting and jeopardizing our future.

With you being so caught up in your own world, you have no idea how loving you causes me great anguish at times. I don't believe that you are intentionally trying to do so, but the truth is that you are! You are punishing me for the wrongs of other men! Whatever your past reasons were for loving them, it was still your decision to become unevenly yoked. While your anger is not always visibly directed towards me, it is, nonetheless, reflected in your attitude towards men in general. I think that it is fair to say that you would object if I compared you to or treated you based on the past women in my life. With that being said, what will it take in order for me to awaken you to realize that the time for change is now? Does something as drastic as me leaving you have to happen in order for you to wake from your slumber? This is not what I want, but if you do not carefully consider my words, then really, what is left for us but to become another failed statistic?

I can accept that, from time to time, you need reassurance that I still love you, because irrational fears come across your mind. However, you must realize that frequent resurfacing of your anxieties and lack of trust can be overbearingly frustrating. It can become so frustrating at times that words that should never be said are spoken in the heat of the moment, and, as you well know, that once said, words can never be taken back. Keep in mind that a constant barrage of insecurities and criticism will not inspire me to want to love you. It grows very wearisome to keep going over the same concerns when sincere attempts were made to satisfy you. I am not at all insensitive to your feelings, but, at some point, you have to learn to get the mastery over your own fears. You cannot always act on each of your feelings, because your heart can be deceptive at times, and it can certainly betray you. Contrary to what you might think, much of the contention between us is a result caused by your fears.

One of your greatest fears is that you never want to openly expose your heart and find yourself at the mercy of a man. Never do you want to experience male domination or find yourself subject to the sensational cravings that have made other women act foolishly. You have reasoned within your heart that it is so much safer to give me just a little bit and then withdraw back into your own world. Can't you see, my love, that the irony in your fear is that you are fighting against your very nature?

The reality is that you really *do* want to give your heart to a man to whom you can entrust your feelings. Open your eyes, and see that I am making every effort to be that man. With all that I have said, I have spoken truth that you can use to bring closure to your past, and that we can use to look ahead to the future. Accept that your past mistakes cannot be changed, and release your anger. You have something far better than the past. You already have in your possession a man who is ready, able, and willing to love you within his means. Yes, it is true that love will always carry a degree of risk that can lead to injury of heart because of our imperfections; but, despite the occasional pains, I am still willing to accept the risks, because I feel that your love is greater in its rewards. I can only hope that one day you will feel the same way about me.

Most people are anxious and lose all their patience
Some things are worth waiting for to make them even better
You have doubts about me, and you need a little time
But, I'll be around when you make up your mind
'Cause I'm sitting here waiting,
Waiting for your love
You're worth the wait to me and a whole lot more
There is no one else for you in this world,
So make up your mind

You might not ever tell me that you're missing my love,
But one day you'll come home to me, knocking at my door,
And I'll let you in with a smile on my face
You're looking for my love and hope you don't have to wait
'Cause I'm sitting here waiting,
Waiting for your love
You're worth the wait to me and a whole lot more
There is no one else for you in this world,
So make up your mind

We're made for each other
I'm always thinking of you
There's no way around it
We can't keep running from the truth
I've tried and I've tried to keep you out of my mind,
But it is up to you to make up your mind

Why do you feel that your love is worth the wait?

The Price of Real Love

How much are you willing to pay for the price of real love? I imagine that you never thought in terms of buying real love for yourself; however, there is a cost involved in obtaining it. Your first challenge is in finding a man with a rich heart and who is willing to allow you to mine the qualities it contains. However, once you discover such a man, his love is available in large quantities; but, how much of it you can actually buy for yourself depends on how much attention you pay to yourself and to the man from whom you wish to purchase it. The buying of real love is purchased with the spirit of your heart and not with dollars and cents. Cultivating qualities such as humility, self-control, patience, and submissiveness are valuable commodities that are very attractive to a man. Bestowing dignity, honor, and respect with a self-sacrificing, considerate, and kind spirit makes you priceless in the eyes of your beholder, such that he is willing to sell his all to acquire you. The purchase of real love flows freely and does not fluctuate in value that results in quarreling, rivalry, and the name-calling evils of self-entitlement. You can buy real love for yourself, but it does not come cheaply.

This type of love is never on sale, and I advise you not to follow the mainstream thinking of selfishness that believes that you can buy real love at a discount. Do not rejoice at so-called shortcuts that promise that you can live the life of true love at a basement-bargain price and not work hard to fulfill your role. It will never happen, because these shortcuts do not exist. You will receive back only that which you put in. Peace of mind and pleasures of love cannot reside in the presence of evil, and absence of love in the mind of a man is also absence of love in his heart. Learn to forgive from your heart, so that you may be forgiven. Live life for someone else, that someone may live life for you. Maintain your balance, and remember that anything worthwhile in life requires effort. For this will always be the basis and the required currency needed to obtain real love.

A Revelation of Life

I used to think that love was a right I had for living, but now I understand that love is a privilege of learning to live life in the right way. When I look back on my past, I have deeper insight, because now I use it as a gauge of progress that tells me who I was and why I have become the person that I am. When I became of age, I thought I had an understanding of life; yet, I was still but a boy in the ways of the world, as I went forth trying to find my way. Every day I was changing. Every day, I was rearranging my life, desiring and aspiring to be better than I was before. It was not perfect by any means, because I felt pain from others and made innocent mistakes that inflicted pain. Progressively, I started to comprehend the relationship between love and life, and, as of today, I still do not want to forget the lessons of my past. I need my pain. I need my sorrow. I need them as much as my joys, for without my discomfort, I would have never realized that I needed to change, and I never would have realized that I have the ability to be more. Without my discomfort, I would never have found the courage to live up to my full potential. So I need *all* of my memories to keep me humble and to keep my appreciation for that which I have.

This revelation came upon me with the same tears and heartache that you, too, have known. The same love, joy, and pain that reside in you, live within me. My revelation is a privilege for another chance at happiness that very few are given in life. I will not waste it because of my pride. It is not too late for me to change my life course by making positive changes within myself. No more will I sulk in the misery of my past mistakes, but I will celebrate the progressive lessons of living that have taught me the connection between life and love. For I have learned that my life is a gift that comes to me from above, and receiving love is just as precious as my life is when I receive it as a gift, instead of viewing it as a right of living.

Memories linger in my mind
Of how time just seems to slip away
The love lost, the love found
How do I live with change?
You are my turning point
Which direction shall you take me?
I'm just a thought away—
Seconds from your heart

Hold On

My love,

I feel so helpless to see you hurting and to know that there is nothing that I can do. I keep asking myself, "Why do I have to be just an ordinary man? Why can't I protect you from feeling the sorrow of this world?" I get so angry in knowing that there is no power within me to stop your pain. I'm not even sure if there is anything that I can say that will make you feel any better. I just know that I have to let you work out your feelings for yourself.

It is not very easy for me to just sit here and wait, because your sorrow deeply affects the way that I feel. I feel this way because I love you so much. As much as I try, I cannot stop thinking about you and feeling the way that I do. I cannot stop wanting to see you smile again and to see you come you out of this darkness. Maybe, I will never be able to understand perfectly what you are going through, but I know that I do not want you to go through it alone. So please, my love, let me be there for you.

I just want to be able to hold your hand and, from time to time, sit in silence with you. I just want to be able to listen to you without expressing my thoughts and, when your tears need to flow, draw you into the warmth of my bosom. I am here for you. I love you. Hold on to me. Hold on to my love, and it will get us through.

From my heart to yours

I knew that one day this time might come
When you would lose your balance and
Wonder if our love is worth fighting for
So today I sacrifice my dignity
I'll bear the blame and endure the pain
To remind you that our love is no longer about you and me
Before God, we made our vow to be a family

My fight is not just for me
But for the sake of what we have become
Two people joined together—made into one
So, before you make the mistake, before it's too late
Go back to the beginning, and remember—
Remember the laughter and how we used to be
Remember the love

A Moment in Time

My love,

Today marks another significant moment in my life. The joy of hearing the news that we are going to have a baby is almost indescribable. I am going to be a father! There have been two milestones in my life. The first was the day I met you. The day of our marriage was the second, and the third milestone will be the day our son or daughter is born.

I can honestly say that each day with you has truly been a blessing. Our journey together continues to be one of hard work. However, it has been satisfying throughout the years. You are an amazing woman in every way that a man can imagine. I feel so honored having you as my wife. Now, I have been blessed to procreate a child with you. Besides having your affection for me, I cannot think of anything else in the world that can compare to this joy.

Although the years seem to go by so fast, it still seems like only yesterday when I first saw the girl that I knew I could love with all my heart. My heart still beats only for you. I am looking forward to the many challenges that await us in raising our child together. I feel that with you by my side, there is no obstacle we cannot overcome. As each day passes, I will continue to look for ways to express my devotion to you, my beautiful wife.

With all my love

Defining the Man of Love™

Part Three

The idea that our love could fail was always a distant thought but one that we took for granted would never befall us. Failure was something that happened to other people. We were invincible! Nothing in this world was ever going to come between us! With all of our confidence, we did not expect that the enemy would be ourselves and that we would destroy one another from within. Our self-confidence turned into arrogance, and the lack of appreciation led us to the point where there seemingly was no way out. The firmer we held on to wanting to prove ourselves right, the more our hearts became unyielding, adamant, and obstinate. Our love had become a literal battlefield, and both of us were suffering from many wounds.

I knew that I still loved you and wanted to end this war. Plaguing my mind were the questions of where and how do I begin to change a situation that seems to be hopeless? Everything that I previously tried had failed. In sheer desperation, I reconsidered a source that had I dismissed on many occasions, because my pride told me to defy it; yet in the end, it became my greatest ally. I finally looked to my *weaknesses* and found that great strength lies within them by allowing you to see my vulnerabilities. So, I humbled myself before you, and this simple act proved stronger than all my other attempts. You started to listen to me, and I started to hear for the first time the despair in your voice; yet, I could also feel that your love was still there. We were just suffering from poisonous reasoning in a battle both of us wanted to win.

In order to win the war, I did the unthinkable. I surrendered! I became agreeable to the minor disagreeable issues! I set aside my pride and *purposely* looked at our issues from your point of view. Although it was going to take time for you to see the changes that I was determined to make within my heart, it did not matter whether you understood at this point—what mattered was that I did. So I persevered, and I started to serve you again, despite the initial resistance that I received from you. I served you not as a slave does his master or as a student does his teacher. Rather, I served you as a husband who affectionately loves his wife, by listening with both of my ears to your concerns. I showed you

with heartfelt devotion that I was sincere in wanting to please you. By using kindness and goodness, the walls of your Jericho fell, as I conquered the fortresses of the enemy within. In time, I became hopeful again, and, instead of relying on my own *wisdom*, I relied on my *faith* more often. Strangely enough, and to my surprise, the love—"the feeling" that I thought was gone—started to come back. It was oh, so good!

Guide Me Into Your Ecstasy

I need you. Sometimes, my pride will not always allow me to say that. Sometimes, I just forget that I should tell you. Remember that I am just a man. It is by design that, in certain respects, your maturity level exceeds mine. You are full of nurturing. You are full of every emotion. You are compassionate and ready to forgive. Remember that you are woman. For my sake, you must continue extending your love to bring balance to my senses, because I need you more often than I am willing to admit.

I need you to teach me to speak love in the language of your choice. I need you to leave me a unique trail to follow which will remind me of your love and the deep respect that you have for me—perhaps a trail of strawberries, covered with chocolate and cream to keep me enticed along the way. For it is not always known to a man the ways in which to navigate through the heart of a woman, in order to reach the stored treasures within her city. For I well know that there are different paths to lead the unworthy away from finding the ecstasy behind the entrance gates. Lead me, please, down into the valley where your tears flow, that I may actually get to know them and call them by name. Guide me along your passageways, and allow me to taste the sweet nectar of your love when it is ripe to flow, that I might discover that your love is my fountain of youth. For I am standing at your entrance gates, because I want to spend my life with you.

When I enter through your gates, I am prepared to travel deep beneath the caverns of your heart. I am prepared to journey where the source of your love illuminates its warmth, so that I can feel the intensity of being in the center of your universe. I am prepared to submit myself to mastering the art of making love to you and to have you instruct me in the ways that the softness of my lips kissing you can send chills

throughout your body. I am prepared for my hands to undergo training to travel along the curvature of your body to touch you tenderly in your delicate places. It is in your ecstasy that I want to hear the whisper and the calling out of my name. It is in your ecstasy that I will find completion as a man. Remember that you are woman. Teach me to benefit myself in your love. Complete me as your perfect man. Guide me within your love's paradise.

Perceive His Spirit of Kindness

E very single day, we have to make decisions that affect the ones we love in our lives. Sometimes it is not always so easy, and we have to face many crossroads in deciding what is the right thing to do. For myself, I needed a reliable standard that could withstand every test of time. So, I decided that kindness would serve as my compass, in order to guide me to do the right thing by you. In choosing kindness as my course of action, I believe that if I always do the kind thing, then I can feel confident in knowing that I am always doing the right thing. For kindness and love are inseparable, and both share qualities that are of the same personality. To know the one is to essentially know the other.

Please understand that the kindness I am referring to goes beyond being merely polite or observing etiquette. I believe kindness in its truest form is part of the surpassing way of love that reaches far into the soul. It is an attitude of consciousness that seeks to add warmth and heartfelt meaning to your life. Everything about it is sincere. In the smallest of details, kindness reflects a quality of love that is thoughtful and considerate of you. Like when I sing softly about the beauty of your love to our baby, as I allow you to sleep undisturbed throughout the night or when I assist you after a meal so that we can enjoy the evening together.

From the very center of love, kindness comes forth like a ripple that extends itself in every direction and considers the thoughts and intentions of your heart, despite the imperfections that may surface. For it is especially extensive during times when you need to express your feelings, but the words do not come out as precisely as they should. In moments such as these, kindness supplies understanding, patience, and forgiveness that enables you to receive the fullness of love in answer.

Out of all the qualities available to me, I selected kindness, because not only is it the only true companion of love, but kindness humbly kneels to *anticipate* whatever you may need. Yes, I have chosen loving-kindness as my scepter of guidance, and, with its strength and honor, I know that I will never have to demand respect from you—I will always command it of you! I will always remain in union with your love. For with my choice, I have taken possession of a rare crown of beauty—a crown that my contemporaries consider weak and contemptible, such that they even make me an object of ridicule. Yet, I am unaffected by

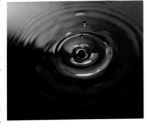

their ranting, because I understand the enlightenment from a source higher than my own thoughts.

The true glory of a man originates from the so-called weaknesses of love, and although other men may despise him, his character is unparalleled in the eyes of his woman. Throughout history, it has been proven that a man can use brute force to subject a woman to his will; however, such force can never match the power that the influence of love wields over her heart. As simplistic as this is, not all men are able to comprehend this wisdom, and I pray that I never lose this state of consciousness and walk alongside them in their mental darkness. If it is weakness for me to be concerned about how my decisions will affect your feelings, then I am a weak man. If it is contemptible to display chivalry and assist you—even without you having to ask me—then I am also a contemptible man. My resolve is not for the approval of others but stems from genuine concern for you. For I believe that, as long as I have the desire to make your life easier, then I know that loving-kindness is still working within me. This is my standard of devotion as we journey ahead, and I want you to take comfort in knowing that I will always believe that showing you continual kindness is not only the *best* way, it is the *right* way for me to love you.

Contemplate His Spirit of Goodness

Come inside my imagination, where new ideas from every sort of goodness come together, that I may bring them to life with one purpose in mind—your happiness. Step inside the heart of my imagination, and you will discover how different teams of thoughts work in harmony to allow me to think about all of your different needs. For my mind is aroused by the feelings of my heart, and, throughout my heart, an ambience of love fills the air with music of songs written about you. Along the walls are pictures that capture the splendor of your beauty: a splendor that fills me with inspiration. In my imagination, it is *all* about you!

Inside of my mind, you have a key that no other woman possesses: a key that unlocks the goodness in my heart. Open it, and you will discover that the goodness in my heart begins with thoughts of how I can take away stress from your life, how I can provide you, the ecstacy of my heart, with comforts of life. Open it, and see that my storehouse is full of wonderful thoughts and ideas to help you, to allure you, and to please you with every sort of imaginable goodness! For my thoughts will never stop listening, learning, and reinventing old ideas to blend them with new  ones. All of my goodness comes from an appreciative heart that is willing to dream—only for you—the impossible dreams.

In my imagination, I believe that I can achieve reality from my dreams. For I had a dream that I heard a voice calling out your name in the heavens and that I came forth as the only man whose love was compatible with your heart. Without hesitation, I volunteered to leave everything that I had behind in order to shower you with affection and reaffirm within your heart that there is still goodness in love. I volunteered to devote my life to the pursuit of your love and happiness. In that very instant, my spirit of love took the form of a dove. My love descended upon your heart, and, as the two bonded with each other, I heard the voice say, "This is my will," and I was instilled with a burning desire to satisfy you until there is no more want in your soul.

Oh, how I do love you. Kiss me, and open your heart to receive my love. Kiss me again and again. Kiss me until passion overwhelms you and the gasp from the soft, distinct cry out of your passion's desperation begs me to give to you all of my goodness. Let go of all your restraints, and feel the intensity of my power bursting inside, as I release my energy into you. As you surrender your everything to me, I will unleash the raging winds from our surging forces coming together, to lift us up into the clouds—where we will make love again, and again, and again.

The Man of Love Does Not Keep Account of the Injury

As time passes, we tend to forget it takes only a moment to say something thoughtless in speech. We forget that it takes only a few seconds to bring to mind a past mistake. Sometimes our actions, no matter how good the intentions are, can cause misunderstandings, which in turn, lead to hurt feelings. It happens to you. It happens to me. However, I know that there still resides in me a spirit that wants to continue to love you, despite the injuries that you have caused me. For I understand that, with imperfection, your misspoken words or acts can leave behind a bad perception, and over time, these bad perceptions can seem to overshadow your good and leave you with many regrets. Yes, moments of regret that make you wish that you could erase all of your mistakes and start over again with me. Although you may wonder if it is possible to start over with a clean slate, you probably want to know how I would respond to such a request.

My answer to you is to prepare a scented footbath that I may place your feet in the warmth of its waters. As you feel the soothing waters, I will ease the tension in your heart, as I reassure you that my love is still stronger than ever. No matter what has come between us, I wash all of your misspoken words and careless actions away, so that my love will indeed prove stronger than any negative feelings that taunt my pride to stand firm against you.

I wash your feet, because I do not view myself as someone of elite status to whom a wrong should never be committed. I make acknowledgement that I suffer from the same imperfections that affect you and that, at times, admitting to a mistake or a wrong can be a difficult thing to do. However, despite the difficulties, I know that the wrong itself becomes secondary to the admission of it. I am acknowledging to you that my love will make allowances for you, because I *want* to believe that you have never intended to do me any harm.

I wash your feet so that I may be at peace with you, and so that you may be able to find strength in your own humility to make your own acknowledgements to me. More than anything else, I still love you, and there is nothing on earth that can separate our love but ourselves. Remember these words, and recall them to me should I ever lose my senses. Yes, I still love you, and you can always start over with me, because all is forgiven. All is completely forgotten.

The Man of Love Rejoices With The Truth

I have always wanted my love for you to possess a freeness of speech that is without hypocrisy or dishonesty, because the seriousness of my love for you means more to me than just the romancing of your feelings. This is the reason that I am striving to show you a surpassing way of love, by living and speaking in the ways of the truth. For truth is the very embodiment of love, such that it casts off every sort of deception and fear, so that those practicing these things may never enter through its temple gates. As for our future, I have envisioned us walking through this entrance, because my love is more than just an affair of a stranger seeking to feel the effects of love with you. My love is genuine, and from its inception, it has rejoiced in the ways of the truth.

In chasteness my love for you was born, and in chasteness it continues to grow. Even in spite of living in a world where deception is prevalent and the pervasiveness to tell less than the truth is acceptable, I reject such behavior! I reject even allowing such thinking to enter my heart, because it is important to me that I keep the innocence in our love. By simply telling you the truth in every occasion of pain or in happiness, it safeguards our innocence and allows us to endure any challenge and survive against the odds. It is for this very reason that my love is flourishing beyond the expectations of those in want of heart, because I am nurturing our love without juggling its values. I am building with you an impregnable wall of trust to surround us, where there is no speaking of half-truths, no deception of how I spend our money, the usage of my time, or the company that I keep. Trust, honesty, and loyalty are the only guardians to whom I will entrust the care of our love. So come, and take my hand. Walk with me inside the courtyard of our temple, where you do not have to seek answers about me outside of me. Every feeling, insecurity, idea, and dream are there for the asking.

No matter what you may ask, telling you the truth is how I will always love you, because I never want you to look at me and wonder who I am. For without the establishment of trust, then what do we really have? Without the continuation of trust, what future can we possibly share? Having truth in our love has intrinsic value, because it allows us to enjoy the tranquility of peace, and it is so liberating that it heightens the experiences of our sensual pleasures. So rejoice with me! Celebrate that having truth in our love lessens your concern and gives you the security to sleep well! Celebrate that we are free of the entanglements that have ensnared so many other hearts! You can even celebrate that having truth in our love is not a dream that we are *awaiting* but that it is a reality of how we are *living*!

Is walking in the truth always going to be easy? No, especially when the truth highlights a situation that is unfavorable or may be very hard for you to accept. Although I will stand with you through whatever may come, it would not be showing you real love if I supported you in an outright fabrication or a wrong rationalization that is serious in nature. The end will never excuse the means, just as an injustice for an injustice does not balance the scale of justice, even if it seems deserving. However, I know that, with imperfection, it feels good to marinate in thinking about avenging yourself, but acting upon such an impulse will give you very little satisfaction in the end. You are better than that, which is why my love will not simply side with you, but will resist you, if necessary, to keep you honest and on the path that will lead to real happiness. So again, I say rejoice with me! Let me shower you with the tender affections of my heart, as you place your confidence in knowing that we are building our love on a solid foundation that was formed out of trust.

A Moment for Reflection

- What price are you willing to pay for real love?
- Why should you view love as a gift rather than as a right for living?
- What are you learning about yourself? What is your revelation?
- Why are good memories a source of strength and encouragement?
- Why does acknowledging our weaknesses give us greater strength?
- How will you teach me to benefit myself in your love?
- Can you teach me without me losing a part of my dignity?
- Should you *expect* me to always know how you want to be loved?
- Why is it important for you to perceive my spirit of kindness?
- Why should kindness be reflected in our attitudes to each other?
- How would you describe the way that I treat other people?
- Why will the way that I treat other people have an effect on you?

WILL YOU SETTLE OUR DIFFERENCES?

The definition of *forgiving* and *forgetting* does not mean that you cannot recall the event, but that you grant pardon without harboring resentment towards the person or discuss the matter again in the future.

- How willing are you to freely forgive and forget my mistakes?
- Why is forgetting mistakes just as important as forgiving?
- Why should we not hold grudges against each other?
- Why should we not keep score of each other's mistakes?
- Why is the admission of a wrong more important than the offense?
- Will I humble myself before you? How do you feel about this?
- Why should you be concerned about my trustworthiness?
- By my being honest with you in all things, how will that make you feel?

- If love is a heritage, how can we show that we appreciate it?
- What is the danger of you becoming haughty and believing that I love you so much that you can _____ ?

(fill in the blank)

- Are you still living in the past by allowing those events to affect you?
- What are your emotional pains?
- What are you so afraid of that is preventing you from letting go?
- Without closure of the past, why will it affect our future?
- Does your past stop you from being the woman of your choosing?
- Do you accept full responsibility for your past decisions?
- Do you ever view yourself as a victim?
- If you want to let go of the past are you willing to:

Not think too much of yourself? (Romans 12:3) Do you feel that your feelings should never be hurt? If so, could you be lacking in humility?

Let go of your resentment and bitterness? (Ephesians 4:31, 32) Do you accept that love comes with the risk of injury? Are you willing to apologize?

Be peaceable and refrain from returning evil? (Romans 12:17-19) Do you treat others like you would like to be treated? Are you thinking about a scheme to cause injury to someone?

Forgive freely, even if you have a just complaint? (Colossians 3:13) Do you exaggerate problems or speak in absolute terms such as "You always ..." or "You never ..."?

Inside Your Heart

- With as much love that you have to give, can you find it in your heart to forgive me for not always loving you the way that you would like to be loved?

- Rekindling our love is important to me. What romantic place would you like to renew our vows?

- What words would you say to me that would reflect your feelings for me?

Choosing a Path

The journey of our love means more than the theme of romancing with boxes of chocolates and red roses. It is a journey of us learning and growing to come to the same oneness of mind. Along our path are different disguises of the same two choices when we reach our forks in the road. We can choose what is in the best interest of each other, or we can choose what is in the best interest for ourselves. It is just that simple. The path of selfishness is more enticing and can even mislead us into thinking that there is justification for acting upon our feelings. The unrealized truth is that it is an insidious trap which has ensnared many couples. In choosing this path, even when it seems that you or I are winning, the reality is that we have already lost. Choosing what is in the best interest of each other is the only true path to happiness, which may seem less glorious at times and is more self-sacrificing, but the rewards are clean, wholesome, and will always leave behind a good conscience.

Our Heritage of Love

Man was created first. It was not good for the man to be alone, so woman was created. Woman was **not** created separately from man. Woman was created **out** of the man. Woman was created **for** the man. Woman was created to **complement** the man, that the **two** should become **one** flesh.

Genesis 2:7-24

This is where our heritage of love begins. This beautiful union between man and woman was the first arrangement of its kind in the universe. Man receives a gift in the form of a wife as a complement to help him in his assignment. The word "complement" means "something that completes or brings to perfection." The spelling of the adjective describing the woman's purpose is with an "e," and not with an "i," to denote that her purpose is not to simply express admiration for the man. Rather, man and woman would enjoy a *dependent* relationship with one another in fulfilling their purposes! This is the beauty. This is the natural order of our heritage, and it is the only basis on which a man and a woman can flourish together and enjoy real happiness as a family.

The structure of the family arrangement is perfect in every respect and if we lose our focus from time to time, we can rebuild appreciation for it by meditating on its conception. It was by divine authority that we were given different gifts and roles, and, accordingly, we should respect and honor one another without feeling a lost sense of self-worth. Only by embracing our heritage of love can we rejuvenate hope, and restore any loss of dignity that we may perceive within our relationship.

Achieving Harmony in Love

The greatest expression of love that a man can make towards his wife besides sacrificing his life is to assume his responsibility as head of his family and provide not only materially but emotionally as well. This is so vitally important that I would be remiss if I did not speak to you about his role in the family arrangement. Unfortunately, overshadowing the topic of a man's headship is the claim of abuse by women due to his domineering disposition or with him taking a non-chalant attitude towards it. Before I continue, let me dispense with the unpleasant and mixed emotions of headship by women. Yes, it is true that some men have abused their headship. Yes, it is true that some men are just outright evil and "good for nothing" as husbands. Yes, it is true that some women have proven to be better decision makers than their husbands are, and finally, it is true that a woman is capable of earning excessively more money than her husband earns. I openly make acknowledgement of these truths in order for you to know that I am sensitive to the problems women have had to endure. What I have to say to you now is too important to allow your defenses to interfere with the message. The message focuses on achieving harmony in love with a *man of maturity* in order to attain oneness of mind. So please, listen very carefully to me.

Although the history of abuse cannot be denied, as a woman, you cannot abandon what is righteous. You cannot abandon what is the natural order of things because headship has not always been exercised properly. If you try to circumvent or defy the natural order, it will only bring you additional emotional pain and suffering. The consequences may not always seem evident at first, but the erosion of happiness starts its process, and failure is inevitable if not course-corrected in time. Despite negative track records, it is still possible for two people committed to each other to achieve harmony in love, if, both are willing to readjust their thinking to reflect the best interest of the other.

Achieving harmony in love to attain oneness of mind requires an intuitive realization of your mate's essence. Maturity in this sense involves more than age, knowledge, or comprehension. It is the mastered appreciation of differences which in turn, provides the ideal platform to grow together to pursue higher expressions of love. A mature couple no longer needs to revisit the fundamental principles of their relationship. The elementary is learned, and their continuation is in pursuit of oneness in love that signifies unity without stifling individuality or initiative. In contrast, the inexperienced couple is unsure of their foundation and wavers in the basic principles of their structure, which leads to frustration in direction, confusion of thought, and the rise of doubts that ultimately damage their relationship. This dysfunctional behavior is always the aftermath of building a relationship upon a foundation without the proper motivation and the elements that will support it.

I submit to you that love and respect are the *fundamental* elements that comprise the structure of a mature foundation, and prior beliefs, the introduction of new ideas, or opinions of every sort are made subject to these two elements. Any vice that jeopardizes the peace of the family, whether it is deceit, overindulgence, infidelity, or otherwise, and any issues falling within the disparaging treatment of one another, whether in communicating or with touch, undermines the support of the foundation. The strength of the foundation lies with building with strong convictions that intertwine love and respect. The effect of doing so bridges the differences between both genders, because it embraces the fullness of their creation and honors each other in ways that reflect true appreciation.

For a man to show appreciation to his wife, it is simply not enough for him to contribute financially, yet disregard her emotional welfare. A mature man embraces the fullness of his woman's love by filling her emotional void. By caressing her feelings with the same tenderness and intimacy as he would her body, he thus makes her feel alive in appreciation both in love and in respect. Similarly, it is simply not enough for a woman to give her love and then neglect to respect the headship of her husband. The mature woman understands that respect means as much to a man as love means to a woman. By considering his weighty obligations and the silent fatigue he feels about failing, allows her to embrace the "logical" qualities of his creation. Thus, she honors him in respectful ways to make him feel the same way that she would like to feel emotionally.

The feelings of sentiment are essentially the same. A woman places emphasis on the manner of love, whereas a man places emphasis on the degree of respect. This is not difficult to understand; however, effectively communicating the importance of balance between love and respect is often an obscurity that is due to selfishness and fallacy of thinking, which persists in women as it does in men. For example, a woman may feel that, before she can respect her husband, he must earn that right. To put this in its proper perspective, you probably would consider it unreasonable thinking for a man to insist upon a woman "earning" the right for him to love her. Likewise, it is fallacy of thinking for a woman to feel that her husband must earn the right of respect. A man has inherited an inalienable right to be respected by his wife, just as it is a woman's inalienable right to have her husband love her. The fact of whether or not one performs to the other's expectations does not negate the right, because these inalienable rights come from above and are effective upon taking the vows of marriage. The fact that *she* is *his wife* is all that is required, and it is not necessary for her to "earn" his love. The fact that *he* is *her husband* is all that is required, and it is not necessary for him to "earn" her respect. Grasping the significance of these principles is essential, because they represent the mortar of the foundation used to achieve harmony in love.

I acknowledged earlier that a woman could sometimes have superior traits over a man. A mature woman wisely navigates her wisdom, money, and abilities in a way that shows *honor* and *deep respect* to her husband. A man who feels disrespected by his wife will not be receptive in responding to her needs. The same holds true when his wife usurps his headship. Instead of listening with a willing ear to her needs, the likelihood exists that he will harbor resentment and will lash out to make her life miserable. In such cases, the mature woman is willing to view matters from her husband's perspective, rather than her own, and ascertains why *he feels* that she is usurping or "taking away" some form of his respect. In turn, she wisely wards off the dark side of his nature by *returning* his respect to him.

Contrary to opinion, a woman who displays deep respect and a submissive spirit is neither inferior nor limited in expressing herself. As a woman, you want your voice heard within the marriage, and it is understandable that you do not want your opinions or ideas ignored. The problem that usually exists for a man with a strong-minded woman is not with her opinions, but in the manner in which she presents them, and, with her not knowing when to yield. It might help if you think in terms of a man who presents you with a bouquet of flowers, and upon giving them to you, he throws them on the table. Similarly, the way you present your concerns does matter in tone, attitude, and voice inflection. Bear in mind that a man favors facts over feelings and that your support of his decisions is pleasing in the eyes of God. For God expresses his love for you through a man's headship, and it is a crown of beauty if you work in concert with the natural order as opposed to resisting it. Be mindful that the principle of headship was not conceived as a form of tyranny to incite male superiority and the condescension of women. It was conceived for harmony! Marriage is a divine institution, and the headship arrangement is a part of that divine structure, because, when it is respected by both parties, it establishes peace and unity in the family. So in conclusion, when a couple unselfishly embraces the principles of love and respect, harmony replaces discord, which enables their spirits to freely intertwine and attain oneness of mind.

The future belongs to us.
Let us walk together. Let us walk in the knowledge of love.

IV.

IN THE END, LOVE PREVAILS

Even In Despair, Love Survives

If you ever feel that your love seems of less value to others, know that it always makes a difference with me, because you are my greatest love story. My sorrow of losing love was so great indeed that I never imagined feeling it again. Yet, when I thought my love had died, it restored itself to life upon your mouth exhaling into mine.

With my new breath, I swore that my love for you would always survive. It will always live in my heart. I will pass it on into the hearts of our children. I will leave it behind in the minds of others as a remembrance of you. I pledge with all of my might to fulfill in you all the promises of true love and will forfeit my life, if necessary, that you may live to know its joy—the joy of knowing that I have loved no other woman as beautifully as I have loved you.

Only now can I rightfully claim my birthright as an heir of love, because I have come to understand the purpose of your love in relation to my existence and how our love is connected with the universe. I realize that, in a universe filled with spectacular wonders, as a child of love, I contribute to the beauty of its vast creation by merely loving you, with all that I have.

Sometimes we can't help who we fall in love with
But, oh, what a moment it was, when I realized it was you
My mind was at rest, for I had been blessed
To have you come into my life
You need not look for love anymore,
For love has found you within me, and
I know I can love you forever,
Walk with you for an eternity

You see…

I remember what it was like before you came into my life
I often prayed to my God to prepare my heart to receive you
I asked Him to teach me to love you—just the way that He does
I asked Him to never let me forget what my life is like without you
So that I may never take you for granted
So that I may never grow tired of you

That's why…

I know I can love you forever

How would you love me forever?

I have come to understand that you are irreplaceable
And that the time that I have with you is limited
I choose no longer to concern myself with minute matters
That serve only to preoccupy my mind
Yet leave me little time to reflect on you

I am choosing to love you
I am recommitting myself to you
To live my life with your happiness in mind and
Where my wants become secondary to your needs
I don't care what other people may think
I don't care what they have to say
You are my everything, you are my life

It took me almost my lifetime to realize what you really mean to me
I thought for a moment what my life would be like without you, and
The thought was too much for me to bear
I possess knowledge, I have wisdom, and I have power in my life
But I am nothing; I am so incomplete without you

With the time that I have left with you
Maybe I can make us whole again
By healing any wounds that I may have caused
Baby, I'm sorry
I'm sorry that I have taken you for granted
I love you

Missing You

My love,

I find myself missing you. For no apparent reason, I am just missing your presence. This feeling is not as though you have been away from me for a long time. It is more like a feeling of anticipation, because I am longing to feel your warm caresses upon your arrival. At this very moment, I am wondering what you are doing, and I am thinking that, if I concentrate all of my energy on you, it just might be possible for you to hear my thoughts. If you can hear my thoughts, then you already know what I want from you!

As I sit here reflecting on the times that we have shared, it has deepened my appreciation for you. I admit that I have been a little slow in expressing myself lately, but sometimes it takes me a while to fully appreciate the value that you bring to my life. What I have learned by reflecting on you is that I have all that I need in this world. All the other furnishings of my life are of little value to me without you.

Just in case you cannot hear my thoughts, I am writing them down right now, so that I can share them with you later. When you arrive, I am planning to tell you that, although I am a man of few words at times, I love you, and I want you to continue being the centerpiece of my world. I need you so much in my life.

With all my love

You're life itself to me
Why must we wait for tragedy
Before we realize that we're in love
There is no more time to waste
I know that we have fought at times and
I have said mean things, but
If I could choose any woman in this world,
I would come right back to you . . . only you
Forever and ever, I will always be by your side
If I could say what I truly feel, it would be so beautiful
Like I will always love you ... forever

Only death can separate our two hearts
That were forged in flames, that were forged in love
I will wait, even if I cannot follow you
Because no other woman can take your place
For I will always be your man, and
I will give my heart to no other woman but you ... only you
Forever and ever, you will always be my girl
If I could say how I truly feel, it would be, oh, so beautiful
Like I will always love you ... forever

Use your imagination, and express how we would spend forever:

_____
_____
_____
_____
_____
_____
_____
_____
_____
_____
_____
_____
_____
_____
_____
_____
_____
_____
_____
_____
_____
_____
_____
_____
_____
_____

Defining the Man of Love™

Part Four

I said nothing when I noticed that you turned away from the mirror because of your gray hairs and your weight gain was causing you concerns. I said nothing when you watched the younger women at play and silently yearned to return to your days of youth. I understood your fears, and gave you time to yourself so that you could adjust to your aging years. For, I, too, have reflected on my earlier days, and I miss the days of my vigor. However, that time has passed, and I was not going to speak to you about these matters until you knew how I truly felt about you.

Instead of speaking, I did something that I felt was more loving than any words that I could say. I put together a collage of our lives to show you the timeliness of our love. From the beginning, your love has meant so much to me that I kept a journal of the events throughout the years. I wrote the smallest of details down, because I wanted to remember everything about your love. When I presented my gift, I told you to take your time as you journeyed back throughout the years of our lives.

During your journey, I did not speak to you as you watched the slideshow that depicted the different stages of our love. I kept silent as you listened to the songs that I had selected, which was a reflection of how I felt during those years. I even kept silent when you read my journal entries, and, from time to time, I would see you smile to yourself. However, I could not keep silent any longer when you became overwhelmed, and the good sort of tears flowed from your eyes as you came and laid your head inside of my bosom. I whispered to you:

If I could go back, the only thing different that I would do would be to find you earlier in life, so that I could have many more years to spend with you. I am satisfied with my life, and I am content with the woman that I have chosen as my wife. I do not want to try to relive or recreate special moments in my life with some younger woman. It just would not have the same meaning. I see beauty and wisdom of your love for me in your gray hairs. I find that, even with your weight gain, you are still very much exciting to me.

Neither one of us spoke another word until the dawning of the sun came, because we communicated throughout the night with touch and expressions of intimacies as we tenderly made love. Never again did you ever doubt my love for you with the signs of aging, because I would often remind you that I still see the beautiful young woman I fell in love with as a young man.

Confession of Love

By containing my feelings for you, it seems that it dishonors the memories I have of loving you. In fact, the more that I write about you, the more I become alive when I share how I feel for you. It is not a metaphor for me to say that loving you has endless possibilities. Since you have come into my world, all of my moments spent with you have truly been a blessing. You have given my life meaning beyond any words that I could ever write that would accurately describe the sensations I feel. I could say, "I love you," but even those words do not seem sufficient to express how deeply I feel for you. Maybe, just maybe, I am not supposed to be able to. Maybe this feeling is the euphoria of love. I honestly do not know, but after tasting the beauty of your love and experiencing the magnitude of it, I now understand that there is no breadth or depth that can contain the vastness of love itself. I have captured the essence of each moment with you, and it has left me with breathtaking views of your love.

In my moment of clarity, I now know that all of my expressions of love should become like delicate snowflakes, falling ever so gracefully from the heavens, and that there should never be a duplication of its beauty. For it is divine when my love descends upon you in this way, and every beautiful expression really means that I am loving myself more fully when I renew this feeling that I now feel inside of you.

Although I do not presume that I am worthy to write under divine inspiration, I cannot fathom that it is through my own wisdom alone that I could begin to grasp the enormity of loving you in such a way. Somehow, I just know inwardly that this is right, because within my presence, I can feel this dynamic energy surging. I can feel that I am becoming remarkably powerful in God's image as I use my thoughts to glorify all that you mean to me! Without question, you are my woman of choice, and I will exalt you in the midst of all sorts of men, from the young boy to the old man, to the weak man and to the mighty man! I will praise your name above all other women in the assembly of them, because I know the profoundness of your love. I know that your love is a motivating force in my life, and it moves my heart to speak fearlessly about all of your beautiful ways! For I am moved by the striking qualities that I have seen coming forth from your heart, and I can no longer contain how passionately I feel about you.

You are my precious weaker vessel. You are my capable, faithful, and lovely companion. If it were possible in some way that I could have a seat among the greatest of all poets, I would speak about how your love has affected me. I would speak from my heart words composed from loving you that I will pen so other men can read, but few may fully understand, until they can experience what I have shared with you. I would say to the poets:

I know of love. I have embraced it. I have been comforted by it, and I have longed for it. It makes me who I am today, and I am not afraid. The better part of me is yet to come, for the man of yesterday has faded from existence. Refined, he came forth as a new man of stature, a man versed in the intricacies of his woman's love.

Examine His Spirit of Faith

The faith that I have in receiving an assured expectation of everlasting life is the same faith I believed would lead me to you. Although I did not even know your name or when you would arrive in my life, I exercised faith in you. I have lived my life as though your love were already in existence for me, although I could not touch you with my hands or hold you within my arms. I used our time apart to prepare my heart in ways of righteousness, in order that, when our moment arrived, I would be ready to receive you as a man guided by principles of love. For I believed that receiving your love would far outweigh the emotional wait that I was to endure. Indeed, this has proven to be true, and my faith in love was reaffirmed upon meeting you.

When I first saw you, every sound but your voice ceased to exist, and the people surrounding you were blurred from my sight. In your voice, I heard the gentle and respectful nature of your soul, and the intelligence of a woman that could fill the void in my life. In that moment, my emotions flooded my senses, such that I became excited beyond restraint, and the strength within my body left me as I gazed in awe upon you. For in my eyes, you were flawless in your imperfection, and everything I could ever hope for was standing before my eyes. Your magnificence validated the very reasons for my faith, and, in due season, my Rewarder blessed me by opening your heart to receive me.

When I received you as my blessing, I did not come to you empty-handed, nor did I approach you alone. I put my faith in God into my love to thwart those who would stand against me and to motivate you to yield towards me. For I believed that you could not withstand the might of a man who uses love as his sword and his shield. Nor did I believe that you could resist the man who uses his faith in love as the symbol of his headship. Your deliverance unto me was not a mere coincidence, and, upon my heavenly inspection, I wanted to be found deserving of having your heart entrusted within my care. For I value my guardianship, and each day I strive to live up to my love through my faith.

Every day, I have the pleasure of assigning you an honor of love that will build you up to embrace submissiveness and wrap your heart within its care. The displays of my affection are like living witnesses that life flows from my love. Just as breathing is important to my life, so is romancing important to me in sustaining your love. For making love to you is more than just an act of a three-letter word. It is an emotional bond of closeness which extends itself for days, with foreplay designed to free your mind to reach peaks of mountains and valleys of pure intimacies. When I speak of my faith in loving you, it is not by my strength alone that I can succeed, but I rely on the wisdom of the One who said, "The two shall become as one." For there is no greater source, except through Him from which I can draw strength to love you. It is only by means of His strength that I can have the power to not just love you, but to *adore* you, in the twilight years of your life!

I have conceded with faith that only God knows best how to love you. By allowing God's knowledge of love to flow as my blood through my heart, I know that you will have no fear in loving me with all that you have. It is God's will for your love to be this way, because there is no future for you in loving a man who will not submit to our God! Before I knew you, I accepted Him, and I allowed the molding of my heart to conform to a higher standard of love. I also accepted with faith that God's standard of love is not only the *best* way for me to love you, it is the *only* way.

Recognize His Spirit of Mildness

I want to inspire you to love me forever, but, in order to do so, I know that your love for me cannot continue indefinitely by romance alone. Romance certainly has its place and will stimulate the erotic desires of your heart; but, once the sensual craving is satisfied, your love will need fulfilling beyond the desires of its passion. I believe that I can fulfill those needs and provide you with security in love, because I have a mild temperament that is well balanced and moderate in habits.

Having a mild spirit is neither spineless nor a weakness in character but is actually a courage, in that it does not allow others to easily rile my temper or cause me to lose my senses. In balancing my day-to-day love for you with mildness, I believe that I can make a positive difference in how you love me. In fact, I plan to shape that difference by showing you the contrast between a man who pretends to love you versus a man who really does. The pretentious man repels you with harshness, bickering, and other flagrant acts of desperation. In comparison, I use soundness of mind as a pleasant way to draw you to me, so that the feelings of my love is as refreshing as drinking water from the well of an oasis.

The difference in the way that I love is no mirage. I weigh my decisions carefully so that you can have confidence in my abilities when I approach problem-solving, budgeting, and planning issues. I have the sensibility to confer with you, and I recognize the need to prioritize my obligations. So while you do need material support, emotional and spiritual activities are just as important and will be included in our family schedule.

When I consider your emotional welfare, moderation in my habits helps me to be reasonable with my time. I will not neglect you by spending too much of my time with special interests and friends or in the alternative, by depriving you of enough room to breathe freely. From time to time, you should enjoy your family and an evening out with your girlfriends, as well as, within our means, the pleasures that women delight in, like shopping, and pampering yourself with manicures and pedicures. These things are important to your emotional well being, and I fully support you in them. I also fully support your overall emotional state by being more than just an observer in your spirituality. I am a willing participant.

I recognize that your soul needs spiritual inspiration to stay healthy. Having mildness fortifies me to stay focused, so that I may not overindulge in any one thing that will prevent me from nurturing our family's spirituality. I hear the voice of your concerns and the need for you to stay in touch with God. This is also a primary concern of mine, because I believe that we should have regular spiritual feedings and make the time to worship together. Doing so strengthens our bond and provides a balance in our lives that will always bring us rich blessings.

Mildness is also a blessing that keeps the excitement alive between us, because I do not have to overindulge in any one thing to compensate for a lack of love. I innovate ideas to sustain our love! By creating the right mix of love and laughter with family, friends, and during our time alone, I make our journey more enjoyable. Thus, our feelings abound more naturally for each other as we feel each success of love. Furthermore, the successes of love that we experience together are measurable, and the spirit of mildness enables me to set markers that I can realistically attain. As such, I have already set within my mind a marker that will tell me when I have succeeded in loving you. My defining moment of success will be when you are able to speak highly of me and know in your heart, that even with all of my imperfections, I am still a man who is truly agreeable to your heart.

Notice His Spirit of Self-control

There looms within my imperfection the temptation to think only about what I want and to make decisions without any regard for you. This temptation to indulge in my own selfish desires can be very subtle in nature; yet, it is a danger that cannot be ignored. To counter my selfish inclinations requires of me a great deal of meditation and self-control. Whereas I desire to treat you accordingly, I am also constantly exposed to worldly forces that keep taunting my soul to think only about what I want. I am fighting very hard not to lose this battle within by reminding myself that abusing my free will will indeed cause irreparable damage to you. So, I am taking steps to avoid becoming an abuser of you by choosing to adhere to a moral and ethical standard of living.

I admit that it is not always easy to practice self-control, due to my inherent imperfections, or to shut out entirely the voices of temptations that are always constantly whispering for me to ignore my boundaries. I know, however, that, for the sake of loving you and myself, I must never stop fighting the inclination to listen to those voices. So I am proactively shielding my heart from those voices by guarding the things that I watch, that I read, that I listen to, and, foremost, whose company I keep. In effect, I am trying to prevent the desensitizing of my conscience, so that a compromising situation thrust upon me without notice will not prove fatal to our relationship. I am also staying mindful of the dangers that other women pose, and that it would be a serious mistake for me to become overconfident and believe that our love makes me impervious to temptation. For the wiles of a determined woman can easily weaken the resolve of a man to remain faithful who is not wary of her seductive ways.

The natural bond of attraction between men and women make the seductress a very serious threat to our relationship. Although I know that nothing good will ever come from her covetousness, I will not underestimate her power of persuasion or the treachery of my own heart. The wisdom from above states, "Let him that thinks he is standing beware that he does not fall." Therefore, it would not be wise for me to try to face her temptations and test my resolve. Nor would it be unmanly of me to avoid or to literally run away from her, if necessary, in order not to become a victim of her seduction.

Unfortunately, I have seen the seductress' victims, and consenting is just not worth losing your respect or my self-respect and destroying the trust within our relationship. I never want to see your heart bleeding from the anguish that comes from infidelity. I never want to see the torment in the eyes of our children or the tears they will shed from feeling they have to choose between us. The momentary pleasure is not worth the destruction of our family, and I will not listen to the seductress' false reasoning that has lulled other men into thinking that an affair is just harmless fun. Thus, the long-term effects of these emotional scars motivate me to avoid all things that could possibly lead me astray and cause me to fall into her snares.

Yes, it will take self-control to develop the stamina to say "no" to *anything* that poses a potential threat to our relationship. It will also take wisdom for me to close the door on temptation, by being determined to solve any problems that we have inside of our relationship, rather than to look for a solution outside of it. No matter what choices may come before me, I have accepted that I have a *relative* freedom to choose, but I do not have *absolute* freedom to do any and everything that I would like. Adhering to moral boundaries is a choice that reflects my respect for our union. My respect translates to love. Although I know that I will fall short in your expectations at times, I still accept the restraints of self-discipline, because, by making the effort, it shows you that I am sincere and that I really do love you.

The Man of Love Bears, Believes, Hopes & Endures

We all relish selecting the mate of our choice and the idea of living happily ever after. Usually, when our dream meets with reality, the beauty of love fades, and we place the failure of it on others, but very seldom do we find any fault with ourselves. In fact, most people are unaware that the failure of their love affairs began long before their relationships were actually started. This is due to the belief within their hearts that they are *entitled* to *receive* love before *giving* it. Thus, their true motive for love is *self-centered,* and, once a relationship becomes infected with this corruption, it will inevitably die, unless the reasoning behind their love is redefined.

Similarly, if my motive for loving you is rooted in selfishness, then it is only a matter of time before my love is exposed for what it really is— a charade. The true spirit of love stems from "I want to" and is not an expectation of serving self, receiving a right of compensation in exchange, or feeling a sense of entitlement that the other person has to respond to my wishes. For if the receiver of my love does not respond favorably and I lash out with jealousy, fits of anger, or if I cut off communication, then from what source did my so-called "love" truly originate? I prove more so that I am a liar to have even uttered the words "I love you"; for how can hatred spring forth from the very heart confessing its love?

When the Originator of Love defined its meaning, he stated *first* that "Love is long-suffering and kind," and ended it by saying that "Love never fails." To begin to comprehend the significance of these words, I reflected on my own personal relationship with God, and I also questioned myself in regard to you. What did I ever do to *deserve* the right to live that I should feel superior and subjugate you to any unkind treatment? Where is my compassion and patience for the circumstances in life that have shaped your personality? How can I remember the pains of my own adversities and then treat you in the same way? I even thought about how I caused my Creator, the very one that I swore to others that I loved, to feel hurt in His heart. Yes, God can feel hurt in his heart (compare Genesis 6:5-8; Psalms 78:36-41). Yet, in light of God's hurt feelings, He has not stopped loving and extending Himself to me. He continues to provide me with the necessities of life when it is within His power to separate the elements and allow the sun to shine and the rain to fall only upon those whom He deems grateful. Even in spite of my transgressions, He repeatedly tries to reach my heart. So, who am I to think so much of myself that I become resentful that you will not always respond favorably to my love? Who am I that I can say to you, "How dare you hurt me!" or "I will never forgive you!"? When I considered the ultimate question, "What if God adopted my attitude and chose not to forgive me?," the answer made me realize that I needed to change.

While I know that I can never display God's manner of love in the same superlative way, I have, nonetheless, chosen to adopt Him as my role model in how I want to love you. I realize that, in order to love you for a lifetime, I must understand the very nature of love for myself, *before* I can share in the fullness of it with you. It is simply not enough for me to want to receive love from you—I have to strive to become the very thing that I want to feel. Therefore, I must transform myself into love! I *must* become a Man of Love™!

My transformation began with an honest evaluation of my reasons for wanting to love you, and, after careful consideration, I was able to fully understand why being long-suffering and kind is stated first in the definition of love. My endurance laced with kindness is needed to sustain you and to fortify our love to bear up under the stresses and the strains that will come upon us. Sickness, financial concerns, and other less-desirable events are a passage of this life upon which my love must expand itself in every season and within every facet of our lives until our love separates at death. Until that shadow befalls us, my love must remain loyal to the woman I prayed for, shed tears with, and through God's *undeserved kindness*, was blessed to share intimacies with in this life.

Having appreciation for this *undeserved kindness* is the reason "Love never fails." When I view love as being more about you instead of me, my love will have greater flexibility. My love will never fail to give you the benefit of the doubt, nor will it worry with undue suspicion. Otherwise, would not our love wither away if I replaced the virtues of my hope with the anticipation of fear? I am not being naïve, but optimistic, since situations do occur that may not always be what they appear. Indeed, by being appreciative, my love will never fail to be strong in its feelings; but, with all of its strength, it will still prove to be as soft as a baby towards you.

Having appreciation also gives me compassionate forethought. So when your beauty fades—I will be there. When all others abandon you—I still will be there. In the very end, I will be the one holding your hand, because true love is answerable unto itself. I will take responsibility for what I have done or, in some cases, for what I have not done. No longer will I place blame on others for the mistakes of my own judgment. Nor will I expect you to be perfect in love, since I have not been perfect in it, either. Instead, I will shift my focus from being a receiver of love to being a benevolent giver of its spirit. It is I who will change my attitude to reflect even more *readiness* to forgive. I will become more *empathic* and more *compassionate*. I, yes I, will open my heart to make peace with all of your imperfections and will refocus my energy on the beauty of your positive traits. For these changes are identifying marks that my love is true; and hopefully, you will find comfort in knowing that I am making them for my own betterment, without any guarantee of receiving anything back from you.

A Moment for Reflection

- As we age, why is it important that we reassure each other?
- How does confessing my love for you make you feel?
- What would you say to the poets about me?
- When you examine my faith, what do you see and hear?
- Do you have faith in my ability to love you?
- Am I the type of man who would support you in your faith?
- How do you feel about my creativity?
- How would you describe my standard of love?
- How do you feel about my spirit of mildness?
- How do you feel about my spirit of self-control?

WILL YOU USE BETTER JUDGMENT?

- Where do you place the blame if you have not found real love?
- Do you judge by appearance only? If so, what have you learned?
- If you select a mate who is so far from your level of maturity, why will you have a difficult time attaining oneness of mind?

- Why does mature love come with conditions? What are yours?

_____

_____

_____

_____

_____

- Imagine for a moment that you can select the perfect man. List 10 qualities about yourself that would inspire him.

1. _____
2. _____
3. _____
4. _____
5. _____
6. _____
7. _____
8. _____
9. _____
10. _____

Fringe Benefits

As a woman, you receive special treatment simply because you are a woman. A gentleman will open the door for you, lift heavy items for you, and allow you to sit down when seats are limited. A gentleman will help you with your car repairs, make himself available in your times of distress, and a host of other things.

Q. Should not a man also enjoy certain privileges, simply because he is a man? What are some ways that you can show honor to him?

My Comfort

I offer you the spirit of my love as a comforter to console your heart with encouragement and to provide you with reassurance for your endurance. I offer you the spirit of my power as a source to nourish your body with my strength of feelings and to open your mind to grasp many new possibilities. Both my love and power are of the same mind, and with one voice, they invite you to draw closer to me, that I may renew your spirit with my tender affection within the comfort of my love. For I know how the past weighs so heavily on your mind. With so many regrets, you want to share your sorrow with a man who is able to sympathize with the woman of your past. You want him to be a forgiving man, who can separate the woman you were from the woman you are today. Yes, I know that secretly you are ashamed about parts of your life from whence you came, and that there exists within you a strong yearning to relive the past. For you desperately want to make amends for all the bad decisions that were made; yet, the hollowness within you causes feelings of despair, in knowing that you cannot erase your mistakes. Now, within your cocoon, you live in a confused state, which is why you are still suffering silently from so much heartache.

Come inside my comfort, and avail yourself of its listening ear. In my confidence, I will soothe away your fears, without passing judgment but compassionately understanding the nature of your tears. For my love freely pardons you and will not recall any of your past mistakes to mind. In my love's comfort, I will set you free, and I will encourage you to live a life of love. I will guide you to teach others on how to forgive and help them to know the tenderness of our God above. For in my prayers, I do mention you by name and ask that blessings should come upon you. For I want you to know kindness, tenderness, and long-lasting peace. I want you to know my comfort, as a comforter to you.

Hope in Love
A message of encouragement

Sometimes, you can do everything right and still not win in love. It does not seem fair, but it happens quite often in life. You might find a small degree of comfort in knowing that everybody who wanted to know the joys of love has felt some heartache. Yes, I know your pain. You are not alone in this respect. I know how it hurts to feel rejection and feel that your love is not good enough. Yes, it hurts to know unfaithfulness when the violator of your trust has ripped through your soul. Indeed, the ending of a relationship can traumatize a person who even has the most fortified spirit.

When your soul is in this state of despair, you are vulnerable to your negative emotions. Rage, guilt, fear, and loneliness will attempt to destroy you and cause you to lose your hope in love. Of course, this feeling of despair was not supposed to happen to you, because, deep inside, you believed that it would be different with you, and that somehow your love would be the exception. You even thought that your love would prove strong enough to overpower him, such that he would always desire to be with you alone. What once seemed simple has become a complicated blur within your mind. Now you want to know the answers to the proverbial questions of "why." You even begin to question the futility of your existence. At the height of your despair, you believe that you are a failure and must admit to yourself that you are just like every other woman and can suffer hurt from someone you love. You feel as if love is hopeless.

As your friend, I will not let you abandon your hope in love. What if you are, in some way, the sole blame for the end of your relationship? Maybe you did make some mistakes, and you did the wrong thing, or you did not say the right thing. So what? It is not the end of the world. What if you share equal blame for the failure of the relationship? It still is not the end of the world. What if you did absolutely nothing to warrant the end of your relationship? Maybe, by his doing so, he did *you* a favor! It is always far better to be alone in peace than to be miserable in a relationship with someone who does not want you. Regardless of the how the relationship ended, what do you do?

My advice is for you to *learn* from the mistakes that you have made and strive never to repeat them again. Pursue peace by talking with lowliness of mind, and acknowledge your mistakes without placing blame. Perhaps your humility will cause him to see you in a more favorable light, which could eventually lead to reconciliation. Regardless of the outcome, you can take comfort in knowing that you did the right thing. If, by chance, you suffer injury by betrayal, then cry your river of tears. Although you will seek many answers, you probably will find that no excuse is going to justify or alleviate the pain in your heart. With that said, now you have to prepare yourself to do two very difficult things. First, you must learn to forgive him, and second, you must learn to forgive yourself in order to be able to move on successfully with your life.

Forgiving him may seem scornful, but it is the only antidote for you to heal properly and to remove any trace of bitterness in your heart. If you do not, you will undermine your hope in love for the rest of your life. Learning to forgive yourself, however, may prove far more difficult than forgiving him. Your self-worth can plummet to an all-time low, and your sorrow or anger can cause you to either withdraw from love completely or to overcompensate by thinking too much of yourself. Although it is true that you always have a choice to whom you give your love, it does not mean that the receiver has the ability or necessarily wants to continue to respond on your desired level. Imperfection resides in all of us, and people's values can change. While it is easier to point the finger, it is much harder to look into the mirror. Familiarity *can* and oftentimes does breed contempt, and as a result, men and women are taking each other for granted and mistreating each other in the same ways. Neither gender is entirely righteous, because you can find selfishness, dishonesty, and unfaithfulness in both.

Now, you can abandon your hope in love by protecting yourself with wrath, bitterness, and by making vehement demands for love and respect. However, those destructive qualities will not yield you the results that you truly desire. Instead, remain under the influence of love and do not allow your negative emotions to control you. Relying on love may seem to expose your vulnerabilites and give the appearance that you are weak; yet, I truly say to you, that you are in fact safer and more powerful than you may think. You see, it is only through love that a complete restoration of your spirit can occur, and your reliance on love signifies faith in God to exact from your estranged mate, *if necessary*, a penitence to the proper degree. So, continue cultivating the fruitages of love, and become powerful in the qualities of submissiveness, humility, and forgiveness. For your power is not in your appearance alone but is manifest from the truths that are contained within your heart. Not all men will respond favorably to your love, and it is *prideful* to believe that they should. Thus, if in your heart you categorize men with a bitter disposition, the *only perception* that you will give to others is that *you* are a combative woman with a biting spirit. Unknowingly, you will also be carrying a sign warning good men to stay away from you. Therefore, be wise and apply the depth of your love to the adage, "Physician, heal thyself."

While love never offers a guarantee of success, failure in love, given our imperfect state, applies only if you refuse to learn from your mistakes, give up entirely, or allow someone else to change your personality for the worse. The momentary loss of love, coupled with anger, sorrow, and loneliness, can overwhelm anyone. So I am reassuring you that there is never any reason for you to apologize for wanting to feel loved and for wanting to love someone. Maybe you will never find that one true love you have longed for all of your life, but that does not mean that you are not worthy to receive such love. None of us was given the promise at birth of finding true love. So while you wait, are you to live your life under a rock? I think not. Get out and expand your circle of living. Think about those who do care about you. Prove to yourself how wonderful your love is by sharing it with others. Go help the sick; extend yourself to others less fortunate than you. By doing so, you will keep your hope in love alive, and you will also start to feel better about yourself.

I am encouraging you to be the best that you can be, not for others, but for yourself. You are a pearl of value. Let no one tell you that you are worthless and that you will never amount to anything of value. Remember that inside of you is where your self-worth begins. Lift your head up, and stand tall. Walk with elegance and grace. Speak in a loving manner to all, and continue to show deep respect to men. For you must never let the better part of your love inside of you die nor allow the sins of another man to extinguish your flame. In honor of you, I am giving you a theme song that celebrates the positive woman I know resides within you. If you would, I want you to repeat, please, these words aloud after me:

"An original woman, that is who I am. There is no substitute for me. I am beautiful. I am wonderful. I can be everything a man hopes for. My name is desire, but he calls me his passion. For I love my man, and I love my family. I have love for myself. I am an original woman, carefree and loving, just being me."

These words represent an inner beauty that every woman should possess. If you are hesitant to speak these words because you do not feel very beautiful or desirable at this moment, let me reassure you that you are. But first, I want to share my feelings about you making changes to your appearance. Cutting your hair during an unpleasant emotional state is not a good thing for you to do. Cutting your hair or making other drastic changes to your appearance may seem to boost your confidence and may even make you feel as though you are making a fresh start. However, most men actually think the hair-cutting ritual takes away from your attractiveness. In most cases, men, besides the one man causing you heartache, would in fact find you very beautiful *just the way you are*! Do not listen to your girlfriends who are sympathizing with you emotionally! Drastic acts based on emotions are like covering a gaping wound only with a bandage: it does not repair your self-esteem damage. If you must, make minor changes first. Once your self-esteem is restored to health, then consider making any major changes. With that said, I will center my last thoughts on reassuring you of your beauty and desirability.

Most people associate the red rose as a preeminent symbol of love. Hence, the red rose can say to the orchid or to the lily, "I am more beautiful than you are." The red rose can even boast its beauty and desirability to its cousins—such as the white or yellow rose—but that does not mean that it is true. In fact, there is no need for comparison. Each flower is beautiful in its own respect, and the desirability ranges in the appreciation of its beholder. Personally, I do not want the same type of red rose that every other man has. I am not going to close my mind to the array of beauty that exists in all women simply because everyone else thinks that red roses are beautiful. The red rose is appealing; however, I will set my own standard of beauty, because I see the exquisite beauty in the orchid, the lily, and the million other variations of flowers. Likewise, I believe that every woman has her own unique form of beauty. Whatever type of flower you may be, I say to you that you should rejoice in your own color, shade, and texture. It has never been necessary for you to appeal to every sort of man. Just be true to yourself, and the beautiful woman within will reflect your true beauty to the one man who will desire you, because your Man of Love™ will be looking at the woman within your heart.

Remember My Love

My Love,

The love of one man can certainly make a difference in the life of a woman. As you reflect on all my words of love, I hope that you can say that I made a positive difference in your life. I hope that you can look back and remember that my love made you feel in a way that you did not think possible. Did you feel life flowing from my love and reaching out beyond the mere words to bond with your soul? If so, how will you remember my love?

If it were solely up to me, I would take all of my creativity, all of my thoughts and energy, and pour them into trying to make you the happiest and the most loved woman on this planet. However, there are limitations imposed by our circumstances that may prevent us from being together. Although some circumstances in life do not allow a man and a woman to be anything other than friends, I know that I do not have to spend a physical lifetime with you in order for you to experience my love.

If this is our case, I can accept my role in your life as a builder of faith to inspire you to reach out for your dreams and to build you up with words of love and encouragement. If part of my assignment in life is to aid you in your time of need, then I willingly and unselfishly accept my role as an anchor to keep you from drifting out into a perilous sea. When I have made you strong, and the time comes for you to take your leave, I hope that you can say that I truly was your best friend. I hope that you will remember that my love respects you, honors you, and will always want the best for you. Whether we remain as friends or cross over a permissible path as lovers, I want to contribute something good to your thoughts so that we may always have mutual feelings of spirit.

I have no idea how long I will remain in the midst of your thoughts, but I recognize that your feelings are not any less real because you cannot express them in ways that you would like. Ideally, we all would like to act upon our feelings without thinking about the consequences, but the experiences of life teach us that we should. However, I want you to remember that it is actually showing extraordinary love to respect moral boundaries or to avoid further damaging an already fragile heart. The nature of receiving true love comes in various forms which are often not discernible at the time, simply because it does not happen in the way that a person thinks it should. I have endeavored to give you such love.

For my part, I do not want to prove myself ungrateful in knowing you as a person by grieving over an unforeseeable future, because I have no assurances that you will be with me tomorrow. I have you right now in my thoughts, and, if tomorrow never comes, what a beautiful day it was in thinking about you. I try to think positively about how thankful I should be just to have known the joy of being a part of your innermost thoughts. Our time spent together, whether it is only for a moment, an hour, or a day is never in vain to me, nor have I ever viewed your affection as something to discard carelessly. Maybe I will never know the joy of spending a physical lifetime with you, but that does not mean that the other offerings of my love are of any less value.

One day I will be completely missing from your circle of thoughts, and, from time to time, something will remind you of me that will cause you to meditate on my expressions of love. I hope that you will fondly remember my love in terms of a loyal friend in whom you can find comfort. Although there is no substitute for a man whispering sweet sensations in your ear, in your quieter moments, you will feel the need at times to read the unspoken thoughts of a man to whom your heart can relate. During those times, I will always be here for you, and I feel honored that you consider my words of love worthy to walk within the garden of your heart.

I leave you with one last thought and a promise that I make before my God. Should the heavens smile down on me with favor and deliver you into my arms, I will call upon the Almighty to transform me into your definition of love, so that I can cherish every twilight moment spent with you. No matter the passage of time, I will always remember that I have the privilege, the honor, and the distinct pleasure of loving the beautiful mind and body of a remarkable woman. I hope that my love is deserving of your respect. I hope that you will consider me one day as a Man of Love™. I leave you with warm hugs and kisses.

Return to Me

Whenever you feel the need to hear words of love and encourage-ment, I will always be here within these pages to remind you how love should feel. Before I relinquish my role as the spokesman of a man desiring to love you, I want to thank you for accepting my invitation. Overall, I hope that, in some way, you found beauty in my writings that left you with warm thoughts, a sense of inspiration within yourself, and a renewed confidence in a man's ability to love.

As I leave you, remember that the knowledge of love goes beyond the mere reciting of words, displays of affection, or the determination of right and wrong. Look beyond these feelings, and you will find a place where you will find rest from your long quest for love. Indeed, you can attain oneness with a like-minded mate, and it is not required that either of you perform some heroic feat. The "sacred secret" of love has al-ways been in seeking the *advantage* of your mate and having the humility of not thinking too much or too little of yourself. It is just that simple. Yet, the sacred secret paralyzes the fearful heart, and it eludes the selfish and haughty to comprehend that only in the wake of our weaknesses can we perfect love and live the life for which we were created.

There are so many other things left that I could say, but instead of writ-ing more, I am going to give you the final word by asking you to share your thoughts with me. So how would you answer if someone asked you, "How would you define your Man of Love™"? The answer to this question is for you to determine, ultimately, but I hope that I have given you enough encouragement to search deep within your definition. I look forward to hearing your thoughts, and I wish you much love in your life. Until you come back to me, remember my love.

How do you define your Man of Love™?

Sharing Your Thoughts of Love

What did the journey mean for you? I am very interested in hearing your thoughts! I would like to use selected comments from satisfied readers to tell others about this book. Although I am not able to respond to every letter received, I do appreciate you sharing your thoughts about how reading this book has made you feel. If you also have any suggestions on what you would like me to write about in a possible sequel, please let me know.

Visit me online at www.kennedyjones.net. You can send your thoughts to me by posting your comments online, or, if you still enjoy the personal touch of writing by hand, you can snail mail me at my mailing address listed on the website. Whichever method you prefer, I thank you in advance for taking the time to write.

Referrals & Additional Books

If you enjoyed reading this book, please tell all of your friends, associates, and co-workers about it. If you would like to send your family members or friends this book as a gift, you can order additional books online as well. Your referrals and patronage are appreciated.

About the Author

I may just be the guy standing in a line conversing with you. I may just be the guy who asks if you are dining alone in a restaurant. I may even be the guy who stutters when meeting you for the first time. You see, I can be anywhere, because you just never know when we may meet. If you were to see me walking down the street, you probably would think that I am just an ordinary man. Truthfully, I am just that on the outside, but inside, I am much more. Get to know me before judging me prematurely. You can be cautious, but, if you are approachable, you just might be pleasantly surprised that I am closer than you think. Like me, your "Kennedy" will not be adorned in shining armor or wearing a red cape, but more than likely will be dressed down, perhaps wearing a tee shirt with jeans. You can, however, always recognize me by my warmth and smile, for that is part of my personal style. For I will always extend my trueness to you, and it is this very same spirit of mine that speaks to you in this book.

I speak to you not as a scholar of psychology, but from the heart of a man who has known the joys, heartaches, and disappointments of love. Thus, my heart knows the same emotional turmoil that you have known. Therefore, when I write about the affairs of love, I articulate the feelings of the heart and the romanticism that has always been a part of it. The only viable difference between us is that I am male; but, despite my gender, I can provide you with a unique perspective on love. In looking back, this book is a signature of my personality such that, if you were a close friend of mine, you would expect to receive something of this caliber from me. *Unspoken Thoughts of a Man* ™ is my expression of creativity, and I wrote it with good intentions of heart. I hope that you will receive it in the same spirit in which it was written. I also hope that you will enjoy it for many years to come.

What Women Are Saying . . .

Carmen W. – Kansas City, MO: "Like the arms of a lover, this book embraces the very heart of a woman. It reminds me how true love is supposed to feel. It shows how to nourish a relationship and lovingly sustain it to reach its full potential."

REVIEWS

Nikki Giovanni, Poet – Blacksburg, VA: "What a treasure *Unspoken Thoughts of a Man* is. Didn't you ever really wish you could sneak inside his head and heart to see what he was really thinking and feeling. Well Kennedy Jones lets us in and we don't have to sneak. It's like talking with your big brother or very best friend or your special uncle who always understood. The tone has the feel of old spice or bay rum. Familiar comforting clearly masculine. This is a must read and reread and read again."

Delores G. – Brooklyn, NY: "This book is truly captivating and inspirational! The words will touch the hearts and lives of every person who reads it and will cause you to look deep into your inner soul to feel what both a man and a woman feels. It will also make you reevaluate your own relationship. This is a well-written and thought-out book by a truly gifted man who understands the needs and wants of women. I rate this book 5 stars. Everyone should read this book to feel its fire and enjoy its heat."

Gayle T. – Roanoke, VA: "My feelings are awakened to be a woman in love. I feel motivated to be a woman whom a man like this could love, and his thoughts helped me to take a look at my own shortcomings. I feel chills because his words are not only therapeutic, but very powerful as well! "

Debra G. – Atlanta, GA: "I feel alive, desirable, and comforted. It makes me feel good to know that a man truly understands how to love. I feel so many emotions from your poetry. I feel overwhelmed. It plays with my imagination. I feel as if you are talking to me."

Veronica H. – Topeka, KS: "It made me feel vulnerable. It was as if you had gotten inside of my head, and you were reading my thoughts—a man writing down the feelings of a woman; it was like seeing myself on paper. I cried, because the words touched me so deeply."

Margaret C. – Kansas City, MO: "I felt as if the voice of God was speaking through him to me. I was captured by every word, because it reveals the way God wants us to love. It feels divine, because it unblocks my painful heart, it heals my inner spirit, and it lets the sun shine within. Every word is seasoned with love, and it fulfills every longing in my heart—it's just what I have been searching for. Thank you for a timely treasure that brings healing to those who are looking for true love."